A
Dartmoor
Christmas

For Sam, Sadie and H.

A Dartmoor Christmas

AN ANTHOLOGY OF DARTMOOR IN WINTER

Compiled by Simon Butler

HALSGROVE

First published in Great Britain by Halsgrove in 2000

Copyright in this collection © 2000 Simon Butler

British Library Cataloguing-in-Publication Data
A CIP record for this title is available from the British Library

ISBN 1 84114 098 8

HALSGROVE PUBLISHING, MEDIA AND DISTRIBUTION
Halsgrove House
Lower Moor Way
Tiverton, Devon EX16 6SS
Tel: 01884 243242
Fax: 01884 243325
website: www.halsgrove.com

Printed and bound in Great Britain by
MPG Books Ltd, Bodmin

CONTENTS

ACKNOWLEDGEMENTS

The author's thanks are due to Peter Hamilton-Leggett for his help in providing ideas and material for use in this anthology. Thanks also to Bryan Harper for the cover photograph and the picture on page 16.

The extracts are taken from the sources listed below, with special thanks to those contemporary authors who have kindly given permission to include their work:

1, 10, 17, 20, 25, 27, 29, 32, 39, 41, 42, Cecil Torr, *Small Talk at Wreyland*, CUP 1918–23. 2, Beatrice Chase, *Gorse Blossoms from Dartmoor*, Longman 1939. 3, Douglas Gordon, *Dartmoor In All its Moods*, John Murray 1933. 4, 5, 35, 84, William Crossing, *A Hundred Years on Dartmoor*, Devon Books 1987. 6, 18, 38, 46, Rev. Sabine Baring Gould, *A Book of Dartmoor*, Methuen & Co. 1900. 7, Nicholas Carrington, *Dartmoor - A Descriptive Poem* - John Murray 1826. 8, John Prince, *Worthies of Devon* 1701. 9, Robert Burnard, *Dartmoor Pictorial Records*, Devon Books, 1986. 11, 14, 34, 43, Anna Eliza Bray, *The Borders of the Tamar and Tavy*, London 1879. 12, Peter Brears, *The Old Devon Farmhouse*, Devon Books 1998. 13, 26, 28, Judy Chard, *Traditional Devon Recipes*, Devon Books 1988. 15, 16 Gerald Wasley, *Devon in the Great War*, Devon Books 2000. 19, 44, as reported in the *Western Morning News*. 22, *Dartmoor – the Country Magazine*, Winter 1999 issue. 23, William Crossing, *Dartmoor Worker*, David & Charles 1992. 24, 45, Arthur H. Norway, *Highways and Byways in Devon and Cornwall*, Macmillan 1900. 30, W. F. Collier, *The Hound and the Horn*, Halsgrove 2000. 31, Woodhouse Lane, *Dartmoor in Devon and Other Poems*, Bristol 1918. 33, Susan Haughton in, *The Book of Manaton*, Halsgrove 1999. 36, Reg Bellamy, *Postbridge – The Heart of Dartmoor*, Halsgrove 1999. 37, 47, William Crossing, *Gems in a Granite Setting*, Devon Books 1987. 40, Robert Herrick, *Hesperides*, 1848.

If Christmas Day on Monday be,
A great winter that year you'll see.
And full of winds both loud and shrill;
But in summer, truth to tell,
High winds there shall be, and strong,
Full of tempests lasting long;
While battles they shall multiply,
And great plenty of beasts shall die.
They that be born that day, I ween,
They shall be strong each one, and keen.
He shall be found that stealeth aught;
Though thou be sick, thou diest not.

Traditional

Skating at Peck Farm, Lustleigh, in the 1890s.

INTRODUCTION

The most likely comment from a moorland dweller on approaching the subject of winter is almost sure to be 'Well they b'aint what they used to be.' In fact anyone with a decade or so experience of Dartmoor at Christmas time is that it's warm and wet, with no sight of snow expected until February or March, if at all. We blame global warming. But the facts seem to support the view that the vagaries of climatic change are not at all new, and Thomas Shapter, writing in *The Climate of South Devon*, suggests that snow, even in the nineteenth century, was a rarity in the county:

A fall of snow is not of frequent occurrence, and when it does occur, rarely falls in any great quantity, or remains upon the ground above two or three days, excepting on the high lands of the district. These highlands are sometimes covered, perhaps for weeks during the winter season, with a snow so light and scattered as to be scarcely appreciable, yet viewed from a distance giving the impression of a snow-clad country. On some rare occasions, however, the depth of a fall of snow may be to the extent of inches, reaching towards half a foot, with high drifts in certain places. The remarkable snow-storm of January, 1814, for the depth of its drifts and its continuance unthawed upon the ground, stands out as exceptional in the history of the county. In ten years (1825 to 1834 inclusive) the number of days in which snow or sleet fell amounted to sixty-nine, and these were chiefly during the months of January and February. Occasionally in the early days of March the fall is comparatively heavy. During the fall the wind is generally from the north-east, the temperature being only slightly below the freezing point.

Somewhere along the way we have adopted the Victorian view of winters past as portrayed on Christmas cards and in the novels of Charles Dickens. But perhaps even in Dickens' day this was an over-sentimentalised view of Christmas where snow and ice (with muffled skaters) was always present. Cecil Torr in *Small Talk at Wreyland* gives one reason why snows fall later in the year but also implies that winters past were just as capricious as they are now:

Father Christmas should arrive with snow, but seldom has it now: the snow comes with Old Christmas Day in January. Writing on 2 February 1851, my grandfather says: 'Not a flake of snow fell on the Forest of Dartmoor in the month of January: not the oldest man living on the Moor recollects the like before.' On 2 March 1862: 'Well, the old people say there never was a February without snow. There has not been any this year, unless it came Friday night before twelve o'clock. A man that was out about sheep says it did fall before twelve but after eleven: so they still adhere to the old saying. But the others that did not stay up, say that the snow came with March.'

Like many other people of his time, my grandfather was certain that the climate had improved, and he thought he saw the cause. He writes to my father on 22 December 1850: 'I attribute the mildness of the winters and the warmth of the summers to the better state of cultivation of the land draining off the cold stagnant waters that lay about in all directions in my youthful days.' He writes on 23 November 1851: 'The old plan was to have the wheat up in grass at Christmas, as the farmers used to say 'high enough to cover a crow,' but they find now from the altered winters that to till in this month and the next is sufficiently early, and better crops.'

Despite the inference of warmer winters, even in mid Victorian times, the evidence from many of the entries in this anthology points to the popular images of winter on Dartmoor meaning blizzards, snow drifts and beleaguered farms. Anyway, it is an image we all prefer (certainly preferable to thick mist and drizzle) and as Laurie Lee memorably proclaimed: we love falls of snow because they belong to nobody.

As southern England's largest and highest upland region it is hardly surprising that many of the passages in this collection relate to the landscape and the climate around Christmas time. However, the season is also about the traditions of Christmas; the way we do things now and the way they used to be done. But as with any anthology the difficulty is not what to include, but what to leave out, as there are so many anecdotes, stories and legends associated with Dartmoor in winter. The intention therefore has been to produce for the reader a Christmas stocking, with some things familiar and some things surprising as each offering is drawn out in turn.

Thanks for help in the preparation of this work go to Peter Hamilton-Leggett whom I have described elsewhere as 'A Man for All Seasons'. In this case the season is winter and Peter has shown his customary generosity in allowing me shamelessly to raid his archive.

Simon Butler
October 2000

A frosty tree in a winter landscape.

1
THE SNOW KINGDOM

1
Jack Frost

In Small Talk at Wreyland, *Cecil Torr underlines the effect of late frosts on the moor. In letters between his grandfather and father he records:*

He writes to him on 18 June 1851: 'People say that Ashburton Fair is past, and the apples are safe.' People still say that, meaning that all frosts have ceased by the first Thursday in June. But many of these sayings are of earlier date than 1752: the calendar was altered then by cutting out eleven days; and the seasons did not alter with the calendar. Father Christmas should arrive in snow, but seldom has it now: the snow comes with Old Christmas Day in January.

✳

2
King Frost

In her poem 'Winter' the writer Beatrice Chase presents an Edwardian's view of Christmas on Dartmoor.

> Breakfast to the robin's song
> As the red sun rests his chin
> Upon the moor's rim up along,
> And stands there, looking in.
>
> All day he plays a jovial game
> With white King Frost and me,
> His spears he throws with careful aim.
> But Frost and he agree.

He blunts each spear lest it should break
The ice's gleaming fringe
That hangs right round the roof to make
The eaves an amber tinge.

He aims too at the fire of peat
That on the cobbit glows,
Pretending to eclipse its heat
With flames of gold and rose.

But Sun soon tires in winter-time
And goes to sleep his fill
Beneath a blanket of white rime
Upon the southern hill.

The old-gold curtains then we close
To bid the draughts decamp,
I blow the fire until it glows
And light the daffodil lamp.

Then comes on gold-embroidered cloth
The meal that I love most,
The cream with rim of bubble and froth,
Hot tea and buttered toast.

The full moon's cloudless light at last
Our artist souls entice
Outside to see her silver cast
Upon the fringe of ice.

The house has drawn the thatch right down
About her very eyes,
She sleeps beneath the hood of brown
Until the sun shall rise.

3
Arctic Dartmoor

Author Douglas Gordon, writing in the 1930s, gives a marvellous impression of the moor in winter and provides an interesting explanation for the word 'ammil', that peculiar and rarely seen phenomenon of icy weather on Dartmoor.

Dartmoor, being the highest ground in the South, inevitably bears the brunt of the comparatively mild southern winter, and since

> *He who ascends to mountain-tops shall find,*
> *The loftiest peaks most wrapt in clouds and snow.*

it is nothing unusual to leave the lowlands in perfectly mild weather and within the hour move into an atmosphere of iron frost and generally Arctic conditions. The actual snowfall is not heavy, although the hills of necessity whiten more readily than the lower country, and retain their wintry covering for a longer period, while the wilder and most remote parts of the Moor invariably experience more severe weather than the outlying points, although perhaps of lower altitude than the hills more closely bordering upon civilisation. For this reason, the wind that blows from Dartmoor is frequently the cold wind of Devonshire, quite regardless of the compass. At all times when snow-bound the Moor is formidable country, owing mainly to its wide sterility and desolation, and though the terrors of the upland storms have been perhaps somewhat exaggerated in old literature, their rigour and very considerable danger are not to be despised.

The 9th of March, 1891, is still famous in the West as the date of the 'Great Blizzard', which, sweeping up with little warning, raged for thirty-six hours, isolating the Cornish Peninsula and Dartmoor in particular. So intense was the cold which followed the downfall that snow lay upon the hill country until early May, and old farm-labourers have told me that during the spring 'tilling' many of the shaded headlands were still encumbered with deep drifts and could not be ploughed. A neighbour again tells me that, remarkable as it

Snowy Hound Tor glimpsed through blanketed trees, 1999.

may seem, that memorable March, for all its rigour, proved to be the best lambing-season that he ever experienced. His flock, by curious chance, happened to be caught under the lee of an immense holly-hedge over which the driving snowdrift passed, leaving clear ground where the sheep lay, but piling up to form an impassable barrier beyond and around them. Imprisoned in this limited area they required close and constant attention, and for this reason survived the experience with a minimum of loss.

Many isolated farms and hamlets were completely cut off, some of them being virtually unapproachable for a matter of three weeks or more. Mr Richard Dunning of Throwleigh, who was then Way-Warden of the district – an honorary office that has since lapsed – found himself under the necessity of requisitioning the services of a gang of men to cut a passage a mile and a half long through seven feet of snow, to enable a couple, whose passage had been booked to Canada, to walk from Murchington to Throwleigh Church to be married. This was only one of many unusual experiences still remembered in the neighbourhood.

This particular blizzard for some reason has acquired an outstanding fame, although, according to existing records, it appears to have been no more severe than one which occurred in January, 1881, or another which swept Southern England on Boxing Day, 1886. Apart from these memorable instances, blizzards upon a less-outstanding scale are by no means uncommon, the storm experienced in February, 1929, being one of the most severe within recent years. Upon few previous occasions has the Snow King spread his mantle so thickly over the high moors, and seldom before have the beasts and birds, whose lot it is to pick a living upon the windswept mountain slopes, endured greater privations, since during the days of the Great Blizzard both cover and herbage were less scanty. It is at such times that the value of tall heather is demonstrated, since there are always areas where the ling-tips protrude from even the deepest snow, and this provides at least a measure of sustenance to starving sheep and cattle, and an effectual screen from the freezing blasts for birds such as grouse or black game. One man in the Yelverton district picked up as many as seven red grouse one morning, all frozen to death within a short distance of one another in a hollow where most of the birds of the district had presumably packed for shelter.

During this period considerable numbers of redwings were also found, having perished for similar reasons. It is somewhat surprising that these birds should remain in the country under such conditions, when even the indigenous ring-ouzel has sought more congenial winter quarters. One might naturally suppose that the redwings, coming as they do from northern lands, would be impelled by the same instinct to continue their migration at least to regions better adapted to their requirements. Members of the thrush family always appear to suffer greater hardship than most birds during severe weather, being mainly insectivorous, and a prolonged frost of unwonted severity is apt to take a heavy toll of song-thrushes and also of woodlarks, whose present scarcity in many moorland districts is attributed to this same frost of 1929.

A sparse carpeting of grass under the snow is of little value to cattle under such conditions. Both sheep and ponies will scrape for pasturage like deer in a similar case, but this is too lengthy a proceeding and the returns too negligible to keep starvation at bay, and while there are usually slopes upon which the herbage is whittled clear of snow by the wild winds, cattle more often than not shun such exposed altitudes. Those same winds, wailing across from Siberia, strike somewhat too keenly two thousand feet above sea-level to permit even hill sheep to browse in comfort. The animals are constrained to seek shelter in the coombes where they soon become engulfed in the drifts. Wonder is frequently expressed as to the manner in which entire flocks of sheep become buried upon such occasions, though in reality nothing could be simpler. As the pasture whitens under the fast-flying flakes, and the animals can no longer feed in comfort, they withdraw by common consent to the most sheltered spot in the neighbourhood, and there huddle together for greater warmth, while the snow whirls and eddies around them, rapidly covering first the hollow or bank behind which they are sheltering and in due course the animals themselves. In a few hours they become entombed in a veritable snow-cave, from which they are quite incapable of extricating themselves.

Animals in such a case never die actually from cold, the great white mantle effectually protecting them from the bitter winds, and at the same time keeping in the warmth of their own bodies which is all that they require. The deeper the snow, the warmer the covering. Wild creatures very quickly discover this, and when snow lies long, even birds take to roosting upon the ground under sheltered banks rather than upon the bare boughs where they might literally freeze on their perches. An animal is in no danger of suffocation when buried under the deepest drift, the warmth of its breath always sufficing to keep a small hole open. 'Beautiful' was the expression of a hill-farmer when describing the state of comfort in which he found his buried flock, and beautifully comfortable both wild and domesticated animals would remain under such conditions but for the all-important question of food.

The moorland sheep-farmer has heavy losses to face at such times, for the death-roll is frequently high. While his flock enjoys the run of almost unlimited pasturage during the summer months – and even throughout the year should the winter prove 'green' – as often as not a spell of severe weather finds him entirely without alternative means of support for his animals. They obviously cannot exist upon the hills, but neither can the owner bring them in, for the simple reason that he has no ground upon which to pasture them. Formerly the farmer, or rather his flock, was protected against such an exigency by the excellent old rule that I have previously mentioned, forbidding any commoner from running more sheep or cattle upon the moors than he could cater for upon his own land should the need arise, thus avoiding any risk of famine among the upland flocks and herds. This rule, though sensible in the main, cut both ways, since it more or less limited the use of the moor pasturage to the larger farmers. It has lapsed, however, and a succession of comparatively mild seasons has induced many smallholders and cottagers to invest their money in sheep, which, winter and summer alike, have to take their chance upon the hills. These are the animals which suffer such untold hardships when cold conditions set in with unusual rigour. Under existing circumstances, there is cause to fear that too many animals in the plight described remain undiscovered and perish miserably in consequence.

There is also another danger to which entombed sheep upon the moorlands are very liable. When hunger becomes acute, the animal naturally struggles to liberate itself. It frequently succeeds in forcing its head through the snow covering, but the task of dragging its heavy body through the aperture proves beyond its powers. The cavity in which it has been lying is no longer preserved by the warmth of its breath, and collapsing round the animal intensifies its predicament. The creature is thus held powerless, and the grim moorland crow or raven is all too quick to note the sheep's distress and its own terrible opportunity. The eyeless corpse discovered by the owner a day or two later only too clearly tells the story of the tragedy.

The chill east wind, 'good for neither man nor beast', must inevitably bring death to many of the weaker creatures, but it is the Frost King's stern satellite Famine which is the real enemy that animals have to dread. Generally speaking, moorland birds fare better than beasts during wintry conditions, it being an easy matter for them to take flight to less barren levels. A blizzard is usually marked by a large incursion of snipe from the frozen upland bogs, and in former years a cold snap was always the forerunner of contingents of golden plover and even black game to the in-country. The red grouse, being strictly resident, are the worst sufferers, owing to the obvious difficulty that they experience in obtaining their natural food, while rabbits, too, are frequently in a sorry case.

After a deep and more or less sudden fall of snow, rabbits make for their burrows if near at hand. If no underground shelter is available, they lie close, like hares, and once warm and comfortable, will not stir until compelled to do so by hunger. Then their troubles begin. In all the sheltered hollows where the best herbage grows, the drifts also lie deepest. They must dig for every mouthful they eat, and at the same time keep a sharp look-out for their enemies, the stoats and the foxes, who now have them at a disadvantage. There are few animals more helpless than hares or rabbits in deep soft snow. The actions of a rabbit in a drift are both ludicrous and pathetic; the little floundering hops, so different from his usual scuttling rush; the miniature cloud of white dust from every briar or fern that he kicks in his hurry; and the sudden bewildering turns which not infrequently baffle the most practised shot. He is woefully aware of his helplessness, for which reason he is naturally unwilling to quit any available cover. Indeed, as often as not, he sits too closely for his own safety, allowing himself to be snapped up by a dog or fox, or to be enveloped within the folds of a net before attempting to move. To the average countryman the catching of a rabbit that is sitting under snow presents no difficulty. He has only to follow the little footprints, detect the round hole in the white surface which betrays the rabbit's whereabouts, and the thing is done. I have seen five or six netted in this manner, or even caught by hand within a short space of time, with no more apparent effort than picking mushrooms. After a really heavy fall they will sometimes remain underground for two or three days, as I have proved by the simple process of studying tracks, and at such times hunger is the one inducement that will move them. Ferrets may do what they please, but their utmost efforts will scarcely dislodge a single rabbit, as many a half-frozen sportsman discovers to his cost. When wintry conditions continue for some days and rabbits become more or less acclimatized, they bolt more readily, but seldom really well when snow lies deep, though by a curious and quite unaccountable convention, such is the time selected above all others for ferreting.

In the hare's case, snow can only be regarded as the great betrayer, for not only does it reveal her whereabouts, but it also deprives her of her one means of defence—her speed. Her long slender legs sink like stilts at every step, so that when danger threatens she can only plunge helplessly along and is soon exhausted. 'Tracing' hares after a snowfall is a favourite pastime upon Dartmoor among village youths of a certain type, the method employed being both simple and effective. The hare is tracked to her form, and, if possible, shot or netted where she squats. If she escapes, the 'sportsmen' merely follow her trail, knowing that she cannot run far, and soon 'hop' her again. She speedily becomes worn out, and after two or three scares, harelike, throws up the sponge and allows herself to be taken. Incidentally, this practice was, and probably still is, illegal, unless it could by any means be construed as lawful under the provisions of the Ground Game Act. Possibly it is one of the many laws that has lapsed from long disuse. In the table of old game regulations one reads as follows:

14 and 15 Henry VIII, c.10, inflicts a penalty of six shillings and eightpence for tracing and killing a hare in the snow.

The 1st of James I, c.27, inflicts three months' imprisonment on the offender for tracing or coursing a hare in the snow; unless the offending party pay to the churchwardens for the use of the poor, twenty shillings for every hare; or within one month after commitment, become bound, with two sureties, in twenty pounds each, not to offend again in like manner.

It is an open question whether persons other than *bona-fide* occupiers of land might not still be held liable under this statute.

Carnivorous animals such as foxes and stoats are not materially affected by the cold. The fox, indeed, must regard arctic conditions in the light of an exceedingly useful catering for his needs. The inevitable death-toll among sheep and cattle provides him with a plentiful supply of fresh meat; rabbits and hares are more easily procured, and, distance being no object with him, it is usually only a matter of going far enough to get what he wants. How far foxes travel is plainly testified by the snow, and of all places within my knowledge, the great Cranmere bog bears perhaps the best evidence of a fox's tireless activities. The waterways, when frozen, provide him with an ideal transport system, and the multitudinous tracks leading in every direction evince his appreciation of the convenience. Once, between Belstone and Tavy Head, I 'balled', as I considered, fifteen foxes, after making due allowance for the possibility of crossing the same track again and again.

Owing to his wide-ranging habits, the fox is not exposed to quite the same danger as the hare. A certain number, however, are tracked into small burrows and clitters in which, under ordinary circumstances, their presence would never be suspected, their capture so becoming an easy matter. Two were caught in a little ground burrow in Taw Marsh after a slight snowfall a year or so ago.

During the prolonged frost of 1917 a state of general famine prevailed upon the Dartmoor heights. Every pool and swamp was ice-bound. Game practically disappeared, while the hill rabbits perished wholesale, as much, it would seem, from the effects of the intense cold as from starvation. John Bennett picked up an astonishing number that had sought shelter and actually died inside the 'splinterproofs' on the ranges, to which rapacious birds and beasts – always hardier than the vegetarians of the wild – came to prey upon the poor perishing creatures. Carrion crows, ravens and an occasional buzzard were the most regular of the winged visitors. Foxes and stoats were in daily evidence – the latter, by the way, not infrequently turn white upon Dartmoor in midwinter – and there were traces of some other animal whose work he was unable to recognize, nor did he as much as suspect the stranger's identity until one morning, approaching a lonely little splinter-proof under cover of some rocks, he came face to face with an otter emerging from the shelter where presumably it had been feasting. So complete was the surprise, that though his gun was ready to hand, it never occurred to him to use it – a record, surely! The otter, surprised, too, sat erect on its haunches, stared at him for a few intense seconds, then scuttled away into a clitter near by.

Snow upon the high tors presents a beautiful sight. The storm-wind works its wildest fancies upon the bleak lonely heights, and after a blizzard, lovers of the grand and fantastic may feast their eyes upon snow effects rarely excelled in England. Peaty-brown and turbulent as ever, the still unfrozen streams come roaring down from the vast white silence of the hills, their dark channels here and there spanned from boulder to boulder by miniature icebridges, frozen spray from the numberless cascades festooning the rocks and overhanging bushes with glittering ice ornamentations of every shape and form.

Most remarkable, however, of all frost effects upon the Moor is that wonderful product of the Ice Monarch's art known as the 'ammil'. This is witnessed when a rapid thaw after heavy snow is arrested by a sudden fall of the thermometer, or when sharp frost happens to coincide with wintry showers or mists of a peculiarly adhesive nature. The moisture, consolidating upon every twig, leaf, bracken frond or spray of heather, quickly forms an icy sheath over every particle of the plant or branch, sometimes far exceeding in volume the leaf or twig that it encases. A stick little larger than a straw may bear an ice-coat an inch in diameter, and so heavy is the cold covering that an upstanding mountain ash droops its branches literally to earth, like a laburnum or a weeping willow.

Thus every mountain ash or hawthorn upon the slopes or alongside the streams, every little warped larch in the upland spinneys or wind-bitten beech that tops the boundary fences, assumes the form of a glistening old-fashioned lustre; each heather-flanked tor becomes a dazzling diamond glacier. When viewed by the light of a brilliant frosty sunset, the wild rugged landscape presents an appearance of almost unearthly beauty, and when wind-ripples sweep along the hillsides with a sound that suggests the rattling of myriad fairy castanets the impression is as weird as it is unforgettable.

The most recent, and one of the most remarkable examples of this phenomenon that I have witnessed occurred in February, 1929, when even the villagers, who seldom penetrate to the high moors, were enabled to view the spectacle in their own gardens. Such effects are not peculiar to Dartmoor, though sometimes represented as being so, and I have witnessed it upon several occasions in other

The effects of ammil on a gorse bush. A photograph taken in the winter of 1929

moorland districts, though never in quite so impressive a setting.

The name 'ammil' is in itself interesting. Its derivation from 'ammel' or 'amile', the old English form of 'enamel', is obvious, the more so, as, curiously enough, except in this one instance, the word is never used in its old literal sense in the West Country. In Yorkshire, however, it is no uncommon thing to hear, in working-class households, the word 'hammel' applied to enamel kitchen utensils, which leaves little doubt as to the connection.

The beauty of the moorland winter is not, however, its sole characteristic from a human point of view. It has its terrors, too, to which a long tale of fatalities bears tragic witness. The well-known story of Childe the hunter, recounted in every guide-book, might be told with only slight variation of many people whose lives have been lost from exposure to Dartmoor's more savage mood. The recent case of the boy lost in the Princetown district, whose dead body was only recovered after several days' search, is still fresh in local memory. But the danger is for experienced and inexperienced alike. The Moor has indeed claimed the lives of various men born in the very shadow of her peaks. In this village is an orphan child, whose father was one of four caught by a blizzard when crossing the wilds, some miles from a track or human habitation. Helpless in the silent blinding snow which rendered objects only a few feet away invisible, the man became separated from his companions, and so the tragedy occurred. Snow languor, which some of us have tasted, in due course overpowered him, and exposure and bitter cold did the rest.

Indeed, those who know Dartmoor best have perhaps the highest respect for her caprices, and are most keenly alive to her dangerous possibilities.

4
The Fatal storm

In A Hundred Years on Dartmoor, *William Crossing provides a further glimpse of the harsh realities of winter storms – this in the nineteenth century:*

Those who have not witnessed a snowstorm on the moor can scarcely conceive the picture of utter wildness it presents at such a time. Should the wayfarer chance to be overtaken by such with no place of shelter near, the consequences are not unlikely to prove serious; indeed, many instances have occurred of persons perishing when exposed to the relentless fury of a Moorland storm. Miss Sophie Dixon relates how when very young she was shown a large rock beside a track on the Moor, close to which the body of a young man of Plymouth had been found. It was supposed that he had mistaken his way, the ground being covered with snow, and darkness coming on, was unable to proceed further, and lying down was frozen to death.

5
A Schoolmaster's death

In the same work Crossing records a tragic event and emphasises the dangers faced by those who fail to treat moorland storms with due respect:

The sad death of the schoolmaster of the Princetown Prison will be within the recollection of many among the older inhabitants of the district. He called about nine o'clock at night at a cottage near Moor Shop, some two miles from Tavistock, from which town he was returning home. A terrific storm was raging, the snow falling fast, and he was entreated to remain, but fearing, if he did so, his wife would become anxious and imagine he had been lost, he determined to proceed. The next morning his dead body was found in the snow. The occurrence took place nearly forty years ago.

❋

6
Childe the Hunter

A young man caught out at night in a fearful storm, kills his steed and hides within its carcase to keep warm but, dying, writes his last will in blood upon the stones. This wonderful if tragic tale is perhaps the best known of all Dartmoor's legends, and deservedly so. It is a story best told on a winter's night with a storm raging outside – and in front of a blazing fire. Here is the Rev. Baring-Gould's account:

A certain Childe, a hunter, lost his way in winter in this wilderness. Snow fell thick and his horse could go no further.

In darkness blind, he could not find
Where he escape might gain,
Long time he tried, no track espied,
His labours all in vain.
His knife he drew, his horse he slew
As on the ground it lay;

Childe's Tomb.

He cut full deep, therein to creep,
And tarry till the day.

The winds did blow, fast fell the snow,
And darker grew the night,
Then well he wot, he hope might not
Again to see the light.

So with his finger dipp'd in blood,
He scrabbled on the stones –
This is my will, God it fulfil,
And buried be my bones.
Whoe'er it be that findeth me,
And brings me to a grave;
The lands that now to me belong
In Plymstock he shall have.

The story goes on to say that when the monks of Buckfast heard of this they made ready to transport the body to their monastery. But the monks of Tavistock were beforehand with them; they threw a bridge over the Tavy, ever after called Guile Bridge, and carried the dead Childe to their abbey. Thenceforth they possessed the Plymstock estate.

The kistvaen is, of course, not Childe's grave, for it is prehistoric, and Childe was not buried there. But the cross may have been set up to mark the spot where he was found. Childe's Cross was quite perfect, standing on a three-stepped pedestal, till in or about 1812, when it was nearly destroyed by the workmen of a Mr. Windeatt, who was building a farmhouse near by. The stones that composed it have, however, been for the most part recovered, and the cross has been restored as well as might be under the circumstances.

※

7
Battling winds

Nicholas Carrington's Dartmoor - A Descriptive Poem *was written in 1826 and was annotated by one W. Burt. The following extract contains references to Childe the Hunter and the storm of 1638 at Widecombe.*

> *How seldom sweeps*
> *The arch of heaven, thus beautiful and bright,*
> *Above the waste! I view the hill sublime*
> *Far distant, lifting in the clear blue air*
> *Its pyramid of rocks; yet oft it wears,*
> *A crown of clouds, whatever season rules*
> *The gloomy changeful months. But when it*
> *wreathes*
> *The snow around its high majestic brow,*
> *And stern the desolating winter reigns,*
> *Be heaven his aid, exposed upon the waste,*
> *Who meets the brutal tempest. Yet, inured*

To cold – to danger, – hardy as the race
That Scotland boasts, – the peasantry who breathe,
Dartmoor, thy piercing gales, unshrinking dare
The storm that would appal the soul of him
Who lives in fields luxurious. On the Moor –
When from the frowning sky the sudden blast
Bursts wild, and thick the feathery flakes descend,
Swift sailing on the howling wind – the swain
Bold treads the fearful path, and through the bog,
Quivering beneath his feet, sagacious winds
To seek some truant of the flock. Alas!
Not always, though inured to hardship-skill'd
To tread with nicest foot where danger lurks,
And brave to face the mountain-storm, escapes
The wary villager. Thrice o'er the earth
Has winter pass'd, since here the peasant boy
Untimely perish'd.[1] *Him the battling winds*
Resistless, and the volleying hail, and snow
O'erwhelming, found upon the unshelter'd heath,
As eve abruptly closed. What woes attend
On pale misfortune's sons! In yonder towns
Voluptuous, the gay, the young, the rich,
Had met, that self-same hour, in many a hall
Of pleasure consecrate; and as around
Stream'd the full flood of radiance, music cheer'd
All hearts within, while horror ruled the night –
The howling night without. Let Luxury hear
And sympathize! as from each love-lit eye
Beam'd rapture, and a thousand angel forms
Were floating in the dance, the wintry drift
Of the bleak desert had inhumed alive
The moorland wanderer; and, as the hours
Of Pleasure's votaries flew on lightning wing,
And strains as of Elysium softly fell
Upon the ear of gaiety, the tide
Of life with him ebb'd slowly, – inch by inch, –
Endurance exquisite, – till drowsy

Death Reluctant closed the scene, and on the gale –
Unwept – unheard – he pour'd his parting groan!
But see, where erst by Piety uprear'd,
A cross, now prostrate, shows the fatal spot
Where fell the luckless hunter.[2]
Crag and cliff, And faithless bog, and swollen impetuous flood,
To him were things familiar; and he dared,
With eagle-eye and lion-heart, the chase
Far o'er the echoing forest.
When the morn Broke o'er the brow of Mistor, loudly peal'd
His merry horn; and, as the red-deer sought
The mazes of the shadowy vale, or swept
Swift o'er the mountain's side, the manly-voice
Of the old English yeoman made the air
Ring with exulting accents. Him the fox
Sagacious shunn'd, and on the wolf, the bear,
He pour'd his gallant pack; till foe on foe
Strew'd the victorious moorland.
Yet he fell Where he had On the gloomy heath
The snow-storm raged terrific.
Long he press'd His noble steed; and well o'er hill and dale,
By treacherous morass, through flashing stream,
And path but dim-descried, that faithful steed
His much loved master bore.
But every track Quick disappear'd; and now the northern gale
More fiercely blew – chilling his heart-blood, till
Benumb'd, bewilder'd, hopeless, and alone,
The mournful eve closed o'er him, and he slept His last; –
the hunter slept!
And oft the swain, When deeply falls the winter night, narrates
To his own rustic circle, seated near
The peat piled hearth, how, in th' involving cloud
Tremendous, flashing forth unusual fires,
Was wrapt the House of Prayer,
 – thy sacred fame Romantic Widdecombe.[3]

Burt's notes to Carrington's poem:

[1] 'The peasant boy Untimely perish'd.' By a ballad, which appeared lately in the *New Monthly Magazine*, entitled 'The Babes on the Moor,' two boys are said to have perished in a snow storm; but this is erroneous. Nearly three years since, two farming lads, belonging to Runnage in the east quarter of Dartmoor, were sent to look after sheep, overtaken by a heavy fall of snow, and benumbed with cold. Their absence being considered as of extraordinary duration, search was made for them, when both were found wrapped in a deep sleep. One of them, by suitable means, was recovered from his lethargy. The other had already sunk into the repose of death. The writer of this was once exposed to a similar storm. But for the guidance of a friend, intimately versed in these desolate wilds, where all marks of roads or footpaths were hidden by the snow, he too, like Childe the hunter and the unfortunate boy, must have become a victim of-the tempest. A storm in Dartmoor bears little resemblance to storms in general. It is awful, perilous, astounding and pitiless, and woe to the stranger, who, in a dark night and without a guide, is forced to encounter it !

[2] Talks about John Childe, of Plymstock

[3] Refers to Romantic Widdecombe and the storm of Oct 21st 1638 when the Church was struck.

✳

8
Widecombe Tragedy

This oft-quoted story of destruction at Widecombe holds more resonance than would be usual for what after all was the natural result of a violent storm. A pious congregation at prayer, sudden death, fire and the stench of brimstone, are the ingredients of a morality tale for which the church of St Pancras will forever be remembered.

In the year of our Lord 1638, Oct 21, being Sunday, and the congregation being gathered together in the parish church of Wydecombe, in the afternoon in service time, there happened a very great darkness, which still encreased to that degree, that they could not see to read: Soon after, a terrible and fearful thunder was heard, like the noise of many great guns, accompanied with dreadful lightning, to

A contemporary drawing relating the events at Widecombe in 1638.

the great amazement of the people; the darkness still encreasing that
they could not see each other; when there presently came such an
extraordinary flame of lightning as filled the church with fire,
smoak, and a loathsome smell like brimstone; a ball of fire came in
likewise at the window, and passed thro' the church, which so
affrighted the congregation, that most of them fell down in their
seats, some upon their knees, others on their faces, and some one
upon another, crying out of burning and scalding, and all giving up
themselves up for dead.

This our Mr George Lyde was in his pulpit, and altho' much
astonished, yet thro' Divine mercy, had no harm: But was a sad spec-
tator of the hurt and sufferings of others, the lightning seizing on his
wife and burning her cloaths and many parts of her body, and
another gentlewoman by her in the same manner; but her maid and
child sitting at the pew door had no hurt; another woman attempt-

ing to run out of the church, had her cloaths set on fire, and was so miserably scorch'd and burn'd that she died the same night. One Mr Mead had his head suddainly struck against the wall in his seat with such violence, that he also died the same night, no other hurt being observed, his son setting by him had no harm. At the same instant, another man had his head cloven, his skull wrent into three pieces, and his brains thrown upon the ground whole; but the hair of his head, thro' the violence of the blow, stuck fast to a pillar near him, where it remained a woful spectacle a long while after. Some seats in the body of the church were turned upside down, yet those who sate in them had little or no hurt. One man going out of the chancel-door, his dog ran before him, who was whirled about toward the door and fell down stark dead, upon which the master stepped back and was preserved.

The church itself was much torn and defaced with the thunder and lightning; a beam whereof breaking in the midst, fell down between the minister and clerk, and hurt neither: The steeple was much wrent; and it was observed where the church was most torn, there the least hurt was done among the people. There was none hurted with the timber or stone, but one maid, who, it was judged, was killed by the fall of a stone; which might easily happen, since stones were thrown down from the steeple as fast as if it had been by a hundred men.

A pinacle of the tower being thrown down, beat thro' into the church: The pillar against which the pulpit stood, being newly whited, was turned black and sulphury. There were in all four persons killed, and sixty-two hurt, divers of them having their linen burnt, tho' their outward garments were not so much as singed. The lightning being passed, and the people in a terrible 'maze, a gentleman in the town stood up and said, 'Neighbours, in the name of God, shall we venture out of the church?' To whom Mr Lyde, the minister, answered, 'Let us make an end with prayer, for it is better to die here than in another place.' But the people looking about them, and seeing the church so terribly wrent and torn over their heads, durst not proceed in the publick devotions, but went out of the church; and at the same time the Bowling Alley, near the church-yard, was turned into pits and heaps, as if it had been plowed.

This story several yet living are able to attest the truth of; which being so strange and unusual an act of Providence, I shall here crave the reader's pardon to inquire in to a few circumstances relating to occurrences of this kind. The cause may be considered two ways, either according to philosophy or divinity.

1. The natural and philosophical cause of such devastations, is thunder and lightning; not thunder (which spends itself chiefly in noise) so much as lightning, which however soft and lambent it may seem to be, is yet of that resistless force and power, where it meets opposition, that it often overturns sturdy oaks, lofty citadels, yea! and the firmest mountains themselves... If any should wonder how it should lighten so much (as often it does) in violent rains; things mixed with and compounded of niter, sulphur, calxviva, and bitumen, may be enkindled by an aspertion of water. We have a clear demonstration hereof, in that which the chymists call phosphorus.

2. As to the theological cause, that is very often the wrath and justice of Almighty God; for 'tis certain, what one truly observes, such dreadful thunders and lightnings don't arise by chance, or the meer motion of matter, nor ought to be referred to pure natural causes; but are sometime produced by the immediate direction of Almighty God; and He may permit evil spirits, who have undoubtedly a great power in the air, their chieftain, in Holy Scripture, being called 'The Prince of the Power of the Air' to raise storms and tempests, and to scatter abroad thunders and lightnings, to mischief what they can the children of men, whose happiness they have envied since they fell from their own... Though the holy angels are often the ministers of God's grace and benefaction to the world, yet we doubt not but that He uses the evil ones as His beadles and lictors, to execute His wrath upon the children of disobedience.

The pious people of this parish (their church being at length repaired) hung up therein, in a votive table for that purpose ordained, a grateful memorial of this wonderful Providence; induced hereunto by that of the Psalmist, quoted in the title of it, 'The merciful and gracious Lord hath so done His marvellous works, that they ought to be had in remembrance.' Wherein is contained a brief history of what then happened, in large verse, consisting of seven feet, too tedious to be hereinserted, though they thus begin.

In token of our thanks to God this table is erected,
Who in a dreadful thunderstorm our persons then protected.

These were written by one Mr Hill of this parish, gent, who was present when this tempest happened.

Mr Lyde (of whom we have been discoursing) wrote also a large copy of verses on this occasion, in English hexameter (a transcript whereof I have by me). They are too many to be hereunto subjoyned, but they thus conclude:

Oh! bless'd be God! for ever bless His name!
Which hath preserv'd us from that burning flame!
Oh! Let the voice of Praise be heard as loud,
As was the thunder breaking through the cloud.
Oh! Let the fire of our devotion flame
As high as heaven, pierce the celestial frame, &c.

Mr Lyde, whom God was pleased thus wonderfully to preserve, lived many years after this, even beyond the Restauration of the church and of the King, Char 2d; and being full of days, he exchanged this painful life for (we hope) a blessed immortality, AD 1673, and lies interred in the chancel of his church at Wydecombe, without any sepulchral monument.

9
The Blizzard of 1891

In more recent times great storms are remembered by the date on which they occurred. Thus the Great Blizzard of 1891 is among the most memorable of that century. It was also among the first to be recorded photographically and Robert Burnard's wonderful images of the Princetown train up to its gears in a snowdrift greatly contribute to our fascination for that event. In his Dartmoor Pictorial Records, *Burnard leaves us with a graphic account of the stranded train and the fate of its passengers:*

Although the fall of snow was not so great as in 1881, the violence of the wind in 1891 rendered the drifts as deep, and caused far more destruction to life and property in certain parts of Devon and Cornwall. The East Dart just below the Clapper Bridge was spanned by such a great drift that persons walked over it from bank to bank. Great banks of snow, some of them fully twenty feet deep, buried up the approaches to some of the moorland cottages; and before the week was out food began to run short, necessitating laborious and almost dangerous journeys to Princetown and other supply centres.

The south-western slopes of Dartmoor received their full share of falling and drifted snow; and it was with considerable misgivings that the train due to leave Princetown at 6.36 p.m., on March 9th, was started in the midst of the storm on its downward journey to Yelverton, with four men and two women passengers, the guard, driver, and fireman, and five bags of mails. One of the passengers, in the course of an interview with a representative of the *Western Daily Mercury* said that immediately on starting 'the snow beat into our compartment through closed doors, ventilators, and windows, so much that in a few minutes I had two inches of snow on my umbrella. We stuffed paper, handkerchiefs, and cloth into every hole or crevice we could find, and this remedied matters a little. The coach we were in was a composite one, of four third-class compartments, one second-class, one first-class, and one guard's van, and we were all in one compartment. Well, the wind was blowing great guns, and we passed through two large drifts just after leaving Princetown, but it required some heavy pulling. We had just been congratulating ourselves on having been lucky in getting so nicely through the storm, when we suddenly stopped, and we knew we had stuck in the snow.'

Although efforts were made to shovel away the snow in front of the engine, it was soon found that all attempts to move forward were useless, and the passengers accepted the inevitable, and prepared themselves for spending the night in the compartment as best they could.

John Butland, the guard, made an attempt to reach Dousland to obtain help, but he had to return to the train, as he could find no direction in the darkness and blinding snow. A miserable night was

The Princetown train was snowed up on 9 March 1891. Burnard took this photograph on 14 March.

spent without food, and when morning broke the gale was still blowing heavily, and the guard and fireman left the train, and after some difficulty reached Dousland.

Meantime, three packers managed to reach the imprisoned train with some refreshments; but all the passengers preferred to remain where they were, rather than face the journey to Dousland. Wednesday morning opened brighter, and the passengers saw with delight a farmer in a field close by rescuing sheep from the snow. They soon attracted his attention, and found that they had been snowed up in Egworthy siding, a shallow cutting a little over two hundred yards away from his homestead, Horsyeat Farm, which lies half a mile north-west of the railway bridge crossing Peek Hill. It is needless to say that Mr. Hilson's hospitality was equal to the occasion, and that the passengers received at his hands every comfort and attention. Although the farm was so near none of the railway servants on the train knew it, nor had Mr. Hilson any notion that human beings were snowed up so close to him for some thirty-six hours. The realisation of this fact will convey to the reader a due

A second photograph taken on 14 March reveals much of the drifted snow has been removed from beside the engine. However the top of the fenceposts appearing through the snow on the right indicate the depth of the snow alongside the track.

appreciation of the fearful character of the weather on the 9th and 10th of March, 1891.

On the 14th, the writer, after a laborious journey, reached the train with some friends and photographed it, one view shewing the lee side, where the snow was accumulated most, and the other, the weather side, which was clearer at the time of the visit. The lee side faced Horsyeat Farm, and as on the 9th and 10th the snow completely covered the engine and carriage on this side, it was quite invisible at the farm, supposing anyone at this point could have seen so far in the blinding storm. As an illustration of the fine and searching character of snow, it was found on the 14th that some of the compartments were filled from floor to rack. It was not until March 17th that a way was cleared from Yelverton, so that the train could be removed, and it took another day to finish the clearing of the line right through to Princetown.

Helping bring water along a makeshift channel following the blizzard of 1891. The frozen up Plymouth leat is on the left of the picture.

On the morning of the 10th, the inhabitants of Plymouth were warned that a water famine was imminent, for it was found that the leat from the Head Weir to Roborough, where the piping commences, was blocked with snow from end to end. On the 11th, Mr. Bellamy, the Borough Surveyor, commenced the operation of clearing a channel for the water; but the prospect of removing the snow was so remote that, in addition to a strong body of labourers, detachments of soldiers had to be employed. Another heavy fall of snow on the night of the 12th, undid much of the good work done; but redoubled efforts eventually triumphed, for on the evening of the 14th water was once more running into the intake at Roborough, and next day the exhausted reservoirs supplying the town were slowly being refilled.

It was a fearfully hard week for all concerned. The brunt fell on Mr. Bellamy. He did his duty in a manner that reflected the utmost credit on his services, and he was ably seconded by an energetic Mayor and Councillors.

It was a fortunate thing for Plymouth that these gentlemen threw their utmost enthusiasm into the work, for the town was beginning to suffer the horrors of a water famine. Had it continued two or three days longer it would have been simply calamitous. The question naturally occurs why a large and wealthy town should be the prey of such clearly preventable circumstances, and one cannot help thinking that should another snow block take place, the patient and longsuffering inhabitants will be obliged to take some desperate course to bring their water administrators to reason.

The illustration, from a photograph taken on the morning of March 14th, shews the narrow channel cut in the snow near Dousland Station, with the water being assisted on its course by one of the numerous labourers posted along the banks of the leat. Behind him, underneath the fallen tree, is the Devonport leat still deeply covered with snow.

2
HEARTH AND HOME

10
Christmas decorations

We think of the Christmas tree as being a centuries old tradition but of course it was introduced by Prince Albert from Germany when he became the husband of Queen Victoria. However, it was a long-standing Devonshire tradition that evergreen be used for decorations. Cecil Torr's Small Talk *contains numerous references to Yuletide customs and refers to a 'German' tree.*

My sister writes to my grandmother, 29 January 1851, 'Brother Henry and I went to a party on Tuesday evening. We danced and saw a magic lantern, and there was a German tree, and many nice things to eat. We enjoyed it all very much, and did not get ill after it.' At that date a Christmas tree was still a novelty, and was called a German tree, as the fashion came from Germany.

✠

11
A chilling night's rest

Mrs Bray's fascinating book The Borders of the Tamar and Tavy *is full of stories and anecdotes and provides one of the best renditions of a winter's tale that has become a Dartmoor classic.*

Well, then, once upon a time, as the old story-books say, there was a gentleman who, mounted on a horse, (at the breaking up of a very hard and long frost, when the roads were only just beginning to be passable) set out in order to cross over Dartmoor. Now, though the thaw had commenced, yet it had not melted the snow-heaps so much as he expected: he got on but slowly, and towards the close of day it began to freeze again. Shades of night were drawing all around him, and the mighty tors, which seemed to grow larger and taller as he paced forward, gradually became enveloped in vapour and in mist, and the traveller with his horse did not know what to do.

To reach Tavistock that night would be impossible, as a fresh snow-storm was fast falling in every direction, and would add but another impediment to the difficulties or dangers of his way. To stay out all night on the cold moor, without shelter or food, must be certain death, and where shelter was to be found somewhat puzzled the brains of our bewildered traveller. In this dilemma he still paced on, and at length he saw at a distance a certain dark object but partially covered with snow. As he drew nearer his heart revived; and his horse, which seemed to understand all the hopes and fears of his master, pricked up his ears and trotted, or rather slid, on a little faster. The discovery which had thus rejoiced the heart of man and beast was not only that of the dark object in question, but also a thick smoke, which rose like a stately column in the frosty air from its roof, and convinced him that what he now beheld must be a cottage.

He presently drew nigh and dismounted; and the rap that he gave with the butt-end of his whip upon the door, was answered by an old woman opening that portal of hope to him and his distresses. He entered and beheld a sturdy peasant, that proved to be the old woman's son, and who sat smoking his pipe over a cheerful and blazing peat fire. The traveller's wants were soon made known. An old outhouse with a litter of straw accommodated the horse, which, it is not unlikely, ate up his bed for the want of a better supper; but this is a point not sufficiently known to be asserted.

Of the affairs of the traveller I can speak with more certainty; and I can state, on the very best authority, that he felt very hungry and wanted a bed. Though there was but one besides the old woman's in the house, the son, who seemed to be a surly fellow, promised to give up his own bed for the convenience of the gentleman; adding that he would himself sleep that night in the old settle by the chimney-corner. The good dame busied herself in preparing such food as

Thick smoke rose like a stately column in the frosty air.

the house could afford for the stranger's supper; and at length he retired to rest. Neither the room nor the bedding were such as promised much comfort to a person accustomed to the luxuries of polished life; but as most things derive their value from comparison, even so did these mean lodgings, for they appeared to him to be possessed of all that heart could desire, when he reflected how narrowly he had escaped being perhaps frozen to death that night on the bleak Moor. Before going to rest he had observed in the chamber a large oak-chest: it was somewhat curious in form and ornament, and had the appearance of being of very great antiquity. He noticed or made some remarks upon it to the old woman, who had lighted him up stairs in order to see that all things in his chamber might be as comfortable as circumstances would admit for his repose. There was something, he thought, shy and odd about the manner of the woman when he observed the chest; and after she was gone he had half a mind to take a peep into it. Had he been a daughter instead of a son of Eve he would most likely have done so; but as it was he forbore, and went to bed as fast as he could.

He felt cold and miserable; and who that does so can ever hope for a sound or refreshing sleep? His was neither the one nor the other, for the woman and the chest haunted him in his dreams; and a hollow sound, as if behind his bed's head, suddenly startled him out of his first sleep, when a circumstance occurred which, like the ominous voice to Macbeth, forbade him to sleep more. As he started up in bed, the first thing he saw was the old chest that had troubled him in his dreams. There it lay in the silvery silence of the moonlight, looking cold and white, and, connected with his dream, a provoking and even alarming object of his curiosity. And then he thought of the hollow sound which seemed to call him from his repose, and the old woman's odd manner when he had talked to her about the chest, and the reserve of her sturdy son, and, in short, the traveller's own imagination supplied a thousand subjects of terror; indeed so active did it now become in these moments of alarm that it gave a tongue to the very silence of the night, and action even to the most inanimate things; for he looked and looked again, till he actually fancied the lid of the chest began to move slowly up before his eyes!

He could endure no more; but, starting from his bed, he rushed forward, grasped the lid with trembling hands, and raised it up at once. Who shall speak his feelings when he beheld what that fatal chest now disclosed? – a human corpse, stiff and cold, lay before his sight! So much was he overcome with the horror of his feelings, that it was with extreme difficulty he could once more reach the bed.

How he passed the rest of the night he scarcely remembered; but one thought, but one fear, possessed and agonized his whole soul. He was in the house of murderers! he was a devoted victim! there was no escape: for where, even if he left the chamber, at such an hour, in such a night, where should he find shelter, on the vast, frozen, and desolate moor? He had no arms, he had no means of flight; for if plunder and murder might be designed, he would not be suffered to pass out, when the young man (now, in his apprehension a common trafficker in the blood of the helpless) slept in the only room below, through which he must pass if he stirred from where he was.

To dwell on the thoughts and feelings of the traveller during that night of terror would be an endless task; rather let me hasten to say

that it was with the utmost thankfulness, and not without some surprise, that he found himself alive and undisturbed by any midnight
assassin, when the sun once more arose and threw the cheerful light
of day over the monotonous desolation of the moor. Under any circumstances, and even in the midst of a desert, there is pleasure and
animation in the morning; like hope in the young heart, it renders
all things beautiful. If such are its effects under ordinary circumstances, what must it have been to our traveller, who hailed the
renewed day as an assurance of renewed safety to his own life? He
determined, however, to hasten away; to pay liberally, but to avoid
doing or saying anything to awaken suspicion.

On descending to the kitchen he found the old woman and her
son busily employed in preparing no other fate for him than that of
a good breakfast; and the son, who the night before was probably
tired out with labour, had now lost what the gentleman fancied to
have been a very surly humour. He gave his guest a country saluta-
tion, and hoping 'his honour' had found good rest, proceeded to
recommend the breakfast in the true spirit, though in a rough
phrase, of honest hospitality; particularly praising the broiled bacon,
as 'mother was reckoned to have a curious hand at salting un in.'

Daylight, civility, and broiled bacon, the traveller now found to
be most excellent remedies against the terrors, both real and otherwise, of his own imagination. The fright had disturbed his nerves,
but the keen air of those high regions, and the savoury smell of a
fine smoking rasher, were great restoratives. And as none but heroes
of the old school of romance ever live without eating, I must say our
gentleman gave convincing proofs that he understood very well the
exercise of the knife and fork. Indeed so much did he feel re-assured
and elevated by the total extinction of all his personal fears, that,
just as the good woman was broiling him another rasher, he out
with the secret of the chest, and let them know that he had been
somewhat surprised by its contents; venturing to ask, in a friendly
tone, for an explanation of so remarkable a circumstance.

'Bless your heart, your honour, "tis nothing at all," said the young
man, ''tis only fayther!'

'Father! your father!' cried the traveller, 'what do you mean?'

'Why you see, your honour,' replied the peasant, 'the snaw being so thick, and making the roads so cledgey-like, when old fayther died, two weeks agon, we couldn't carry un to Tavistock to bury un; and so mother put un in the old box, and salted un in: mother's a fine hand at salting un in.'

Need a word more be said of the traveller and his breakfast; for so powerful was the association of ideas in a mind as imaginative as that of our gentleman, that he now looked with horror upon the smoking rasher, and fancied it nothing less than a slice of 'old fayther.' He got up, paid his lodging, saddled his horse; and quitting the house, where surprise, terror, joy, and disgust had, by turns, so powerfully possessed him, he made his way through every impediment of snow and storm. And never could he afterwards be prevailed upon to touch bacon, since it always brought to mind the painful feelings and recollections connected with the adventure of 'salting un in.'

✳

12
Cottage baking

The Dartmoor cottage had an open fireplace on which most or all of the cooking was done. Built into the side of the hearth was an opening for a bread oven, or a cloam oven, in which bread and pies were cooked. Peter Brears in The Old Devon Farmhouse *explains how baking was done.*

For baking, most houses had an oven built into one corner of the fireplace, usually, but not exclusively, opposite the window, to take advantage of the light. The oven itself took the form of a roughly rectangular or arch-topped doorway leading into a round domed chamber, perhaps up to four feet deep, built into the thickness of the chimney stack. It might be lined with stone on Dartmoor, often with brick in other areas, while to the north and west of the county cloam (pottery) ovens were more common. Made from clay tempered with coarse grit from the river Torridge at Bideford and made in the North Devon potteries, or perhaps from Lake's Pottery at Truro, these came as ready-made units for building into the masonry. As 'a Gentleman' described in his Essays for the Month of December of 1716:

> *The Barnstaple Ovens of Devonshire, which are now made and us'd in some other counties; and first being form'd in Potters Clay in one entire Piece, are not only cleaner and cheaper Than any other Ovens, but bake with more Evenness and Certainty, and consume not a Fourth of the Fuel which is wasted in those of the ordinary Fashion in London and elsewhere.*

In use, a facket o' 'ood (faggot of wood), a blast o' vuzz (blast of furze, i.e gorse), or on moorland farms, turves (peat), was set alight and thrust into the back of the oven using a furze fork. As the fuel burned, its smoke issued from the oven door and was drawn up the chimney. Once the oven was really hot, the ashes were pulled out with a rake, the fine ash mopped up with a wet oven swab or mawkin, and the bread etc. placed inside using a large oven-slice or peel. The oven door, traditionally a loose slab of wood, usually chestnut, fitted with a handle, or a cloam door for a cloam oven, was then placed across the doorway and sealed in place with clay, cob or mortar, but more recent ovens had hinged iron doors, similar to those on industrially-produced kitchen ranges. After perhaps 60 or 70 minutes the baking was complete and, on opening the door, it was drawn out on the peel, and set aside to cool.

As in most parts of upland Britain, there were practical alternatives to heating these large built-in ovens. In Devon, baking on the actual hearth was carried out using a baking kettle, called a wovering pan in West Devon. This involved heating a baking iron, a heavy iron disc, by slipping it under the burning fire. It was then pulled to the side of the hearth, the loaf, cake, or dish of meat and vegetables to be baked placed upon it, and the baking

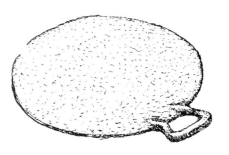

A baking iron

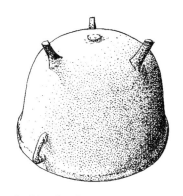

A baking kettle

kettle, a three-legged iron pot, inverted over it. Smouldering turves, fags (surface peats), cinders, ashes, vearns (bracken), leaves, hay, or even dowst (chaff) were then heaped around the kettle, and the whole left to bake slowly for several hours.

In 1750 Dr Richard Pococke had noted that 'in the very western parts they have pot-ovens, a round piece of iron is heated on which the bread is put and is then cover'd over with a pot, on which they heap the embers to keep in the heat'. These pots, or baking kettles, remained in use up to the 1930s, when an old lady at a Poundsgate cottage told Mrs Fielden 'I be gwain to put a' old hen under thic kettle, an' when 'er comes out 'er'll be as tender as a chick!'

A typical open fireplace in a Dartmoor cottage.

48

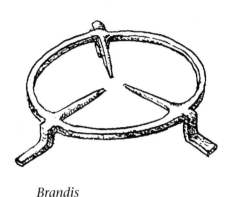

Brandis

Another option was to put the hot baking iron on a very low brandis in the fire on the hearth, place the food on the top, and then cover it with a baker, a vessel like a deep iron frying pan but without the long handle. After being covered with burning fuel, it was left to cook. This method, identical to the *padell r gradell* (pan and griddle) baking of the Lleyn peninsular in North Wales, was still being carried out at Poundsgate in the 1930s.

A further method involved the use of a camp kettle, a broad cylindrical iron pot with three short legs, a hoop handle, a slightly domed lid with a raised rim, and an internal false bottom to prevent the food from burning. In use, this was either stood in the fire, or hung from a hook over the fire, burning fuel being piled on top of the lid to produce a relatively even all-round heat.

✴

13
Cottage baking

Open hearths were just the place to hang a leg of ham in order to smoke it gently over a peat fire. This ancient recipe suggests how:

To make a pork ham:
Hang them a day or two. Then two pounds of salt, two pounds of the coarsest sugar and two ounces of saltpetre, mix altogether, then rub your ham very well and fill the lower part of it with the above. Let it lie a month turning it every day and basting it, then rub it in bread and smoke it a fortnight in wood smoke, then put it into a paper bag and keep it in a damp place before it begins to mould.

✴

14
A Christmas Rose

It is here said,* that if a young woman, on mid summer-day, plucks a full-blown rose blindfolded, while the chimes are playing twelve, and folds it up in a sheet of white paper, and does not open it till Christmas-day, it will then be found as fresh as when gathered; and if she places it in her bosom, the young man to whom she is to be married will come and snatch it away.

* Mrs Bray of Tavistock.

15
Home Front

When the Great War began in 1914 it was said by all that it 'would be over by Christmas.' In fact five savage years of war were to be endured. In his book, Devon in the Great War, Gerald Wasley describes Christmas shopping on the Home Front.

The first wartime Christmas in Devon was celebrated in traditional style with civilians and servicemen sitting down at the table for their Christmas dinner. Whatever the inflated prices there was no shortage of food, unlike the first Christmas of the Second World War when food was officially rationed. Devon shops were full of gifts, for example perfume sprays, cut glass toilet bottles, cigars and pipes were advertised as suggested presents. Family parlour games, piano sheet music and plenty of children's toys were being sold, but the once popular German dolls had disappeared from the toy shops.

An Edwardian child's Christmas dream: a toy car in a Tavistock shop window.

Relatives and friends on active service were not forgotten, with parcels and Christmas cards being received at the Front.

Gerald Wasley describes one of the most remarkable episodes of the First World War that occurred in the trenches at Christmas 1914 when British and German troops for a moment forgot their emnity. Elements of the Devonshire Regiment including many Dartmoor men were present.

16
Christmas Truce

While people at Devon were at home during Christmas, the 1st and 2nd Battalions of the Devonshire Regiment spent Christmas Eve and Christmas Day in the trenches. The 1st Battalion were in water-logged trenches outside the small shell-torn village of Wulvererghem. Christmas Eve was a bitterly cold day with snow-falls. The trenchwater froze. A private of No.4 platoon was killed by a sniper's bullet and within an hour his body was frozen stiff. At 8pm a sentry reported lights showing from the enemy trenches, then a Christmas tree with cards was hoisted from a German trench and fixed on a parapet by enemy soldiers working in full view of the Devons: not a shot was fired. Later, music was heard, then singing by hundreds of German voices. In response the Devons started to sing hymns and carols, each side cheering the other's singing.

Christmas eve for men of the 2nd Battalion of Devons was the most peaceful night of the war so far. They had no proper dug outs at this part of the front line which meant the men sleeping on the frozen trench floor. The following morning, according to routine, the Devons 'stood to', and eventually the order came for the men to stand down. The morning's task was to build up the weakest places in the parapet, the men working with fewer precautions than normally were taken.

Across no man's land the Germans worked on their trenches, standing up in full view of the Devons. Then an unarmed German soldier, a huge man wearing a green uniform, top boots and a spiked helmet slowly walked across to the Devons and called out 'you no shoot, we no shoot, Christmas for both.' Not one man moved, then, as though by command, both sides left their trenches and met in the middle of no man's land. Instead of trying to kill each other they exchanged cigars, regimental buttons and other small souvenirs.

Later in the afternoon a group photograph was taken of some sixty Devons with German soldiers. As the light faded both sides returned to their trenches; the night remained silent. The following morning machine guns from both sides started up, sweeping across the opposing trenches.

17
Christmas Tricks

In Small Talk, *Cecil Torr describes the tricks young men got up to in Victorian times:*

In the old days of practical joking it was one of the stock jokes to go out to some cross-road in the middle of the night, dig up the sign-post, turn it round a right-angle, and fix it down again with its arms all pointing the wrong way. There were two men whom I remember very well – old friends of my father's – and he told me that these two did this on Dartmoor several times, usually in snowstorms, as the snow soon covered up all traces of their work. But he thought the best part of the joke was in their going out on the bleak moorland in the snow to do a thing like that.

✳

18
Bleak House

The construction of a prison to house prisoners-of-war at Princetown was part of Sir Thomas Tyrwhitt's grand design for 'improving' the moor (and to provide cheap labour). Sabine Baring-Gould reflects on the fate of these poor wretches facing a solitary moorland Yuletide.

At his [Tyrwhitt's] recommendation prisons were erected at Princetown in 1806, at a cost of £130,000, for the captives in the French and American wars. Sir George Magrath, M.D., the physician who presided over the medical department from 1814 until the close of the war, testified to the salubrity of the establishment:

Dartmoor prison, Princetown in the early years of the twentieth century. This forbidding place was also the scene of the great Christmas breakout by the 'Mad Axeman' Frank Mitchell who, in December 1966, fled from a working party and literally vanished.

From personal correspondence with other establishments similar to Dartmoor, I presume the statistical record of that great tomb of the living (embosomed as it is in a desert and desolate waste of wild, and in the winter time terrible scenery, exhibiting the sublimity and grandeur occasionally of elemental strife, but never partaking of the beautiful of Nature; its climate, too, cheerless and hyperborean), with all its disadvantages, will show that the health of its incarcerated tenants, in a general way, equalled, if not surpassed, any war prison in England or Scotland. This might be considered an anomaly in sanitary history, when we reflect how ungenially it might be supposed to act on southern constitutions; for it was not unusual in the months of December and January for the thermometer to stand at thirty-three to thirty-five degrees below freezing, indicating cold almost too intense to support animal life. But the density of the congregated numbers in the prison created an artificial climate, which counteracted the torpifying effect of the Russian climate without. Like most climates of extreme heat or cold, the newcomers required a seasoning to assimilate their constitution to its peculiarities, in the progress of which indispositions, incidental to low temperature, assailed them; and it was an everyday occurrence among the reprobate and incorrigible classes of the prisoners, who gambled away their clothing and rations, for individuals to be brought up to the receiving room in a state of suspended animation, from which they were usually resuscitated by the process resorted to in like circumstances in frigid regions. I believe one death only took place during my sojourn at Dartmoor, from torpor induced by cold, and the profligate part of the French were the only sufferers. As soon as the system became acclimated to the region in which they lived, health was seldom disturbed.

✵

19
A Christmas Reward

At Christmas a prisoner's thoughts turned to home. The following stories reveal the misfortunes of two nineteenth-century escapees.

A farmer from Peter Tavy received a surprise gift when he found an escaped prisoner in his yard and, detaining him, claimed a £5 reward. Quite a sum in 1853. This followed a spate of awful weather in which the snowdrifts were so deep on the moor that food supplies could not be brought to the prison at Princetown. The water supply was frozen and prisoner's rations were further reduced when convict John Brown made his escape. Some indication of the desperate conditions inside the prison can be gauged by the truly arctic landscape into which Brown chose to make his break for freedom. After running for several miles across a barren and frozen moor, Brown reached the farm at Peter Tavy where he collapsed. Indeed, so severe was his condition that his return to prison was delayed due to frostbite which required the amputation of several toes.

On Christmas eve 1896 22-year-old William Carter was shot dead as he made a bid for freedom from a working party at Blackabrook.

20
Keep the home fires burning

In Lustleigh a neighbourhood dispute appears to ignore the season of goodwill – as Cecil Torr relates. It is an early example of finding 'something nasty in the woodshed.'

Some eighty years ago a man put an explosive in a log in his woodhouse, and the log exploded on a neighbour's hearth. The woodhouse was inviolate after that, but the neighbour's injuries were serious; and my grandfather doubted if it was fair game. Taking things for personal use is not the same as taking things for pawn or sale; and I have known it done by men who otherwise were straight – except in horse-dealing and flower-shows and other such matters as have ethics of their own.

21
Winter scenes in a Dartmoor village

The enigmatic Beatrice Chase lived at Venton, Widecombe in the Moor where she built a small chapel in which to practise her devotions. Her books record her simple domestic life and the lives of the villagers who dwelt around her. In The Dartmoor Window Again *she provides a glimpse of life during two winters of the Great War period.*

We had two experiences. One was in the early spring of 1916, and the other lasted from the November of that year till the April of 1917.

The first was the most extraordinary, though the shortest. We went to bed one night, as usual not suspecting anything phenomenal in the way of cold, and when I looked out in the morning, I wondered if I was dreaming. The place was unrecognizable. A brisk easterly wind was blowing, which drove before it clouds of white

The author Beatrice Chase (Olive Katharine Parr) at her Dartmoor window.

powder. The moor and tors were as invisible as if it had been a thick mist. At this corner, the high road to the village was built up by a solid white wall, one end of which was ten feet high. Along the bit of common ground in front of the house, there was a vast wall, ten or twelve feet broad and six feet high, built between us and the wind. The gateways of the fields were buried.

Soon after dawn, our farm tenant took his largest horse from the stable, tied a long rope to it, and, himself standing stationary, drove it to and fro through the wall of snow on the road like a snow plough. This broke a narrow exit for man and beast. The air was not extravagantly cold. In time, the snow ceased and the sun came out. The wind dropped, too, and I sallied out to inspect. On the hill leading up from the Webburn to the village, there were drifts and mountains of snow.

Alongside one hedge was a narrow path just wide enough to squeeze through. One squeezed, with an apprehensive look out upon the mountain on the other side. If an avalanche had descended, one could scarcely have emerged alive. The whole of that stretch of banked snow was like extraordinary designs in white coral, rocks and reefs and turrets and icicles of white coral with a roughened surface. I used to take a camp stool and sit under it, studying the wonderful designs. On the big hill to our other side, there was a similar narrow track, but the piled ranges of snow on that road would have filled many train-loads of empty trucks. From there to Cold East Cross was one vast sheet, measuring thousands of acres. It was so deep that the tops of the walls and the tops of the hawthorn trees were entirely buried, and it was fully three weeks before that road was open, even with gangs of men working continually.

Some of the outlying farms and cottages suffered severely for want of food. No bread or yeast could be delivered, and they had to do the best they could with what was in the house.

A few of the drifts were designed like a gigantic shell as large as a small cottage. The effect of this snow-fall was a unique experience.

The peace and brilliance of the moor, covered by such a thick mantle, the feeling that we were practically cut off from civilisation, was a thing not to have missed. No vehicle of any kind could travel. Pony-back or Shank's mare were the only means of locomotion.

We wondered, the first morning, if we should see any mails. Our valiant postman arrived after 11am instead of at 8.15. He was stunned. I never saw a man so nearly exhausted. But he would do the return journey. He told us later that, for the first time in his service life, he had taken back to the office, letters which had been given him to deliver. Some of his haunts were impassable, even if he had not been utterly exhausted.

One interesting thing was to watch all the tracks in the snow on the roads. For a long time, every mark was recorded. One morning, up the big hill, there was a complete chain of rabbit tracks. The rabbit had apparently hopped straight up the middle of the hill, along the snow, in a series of leaps...

The thaw was the most artistic I have ever seen. Usually, a thaw means roads running with icy slush, tears and rents everywhere and all bridges washed bare to their granite ribs. This colossal mass of snow vanished as quietly as the mist, and with no more damage. It was, therefore, a ground thaw. The worst thaws are those that come from above, with heavy rain, before the ground has got warm. Then look out for raging torrents instead of roads. This time, the warmth began underground, and the snow sank in imperceptibly.

The next spell of cold was very different. There was little snow but such wind and frost as I never hope to see and feel again. It began in November and went practically right through to April. The first week of that month, we had heavy snow.

It did one good thing, which was to kill the wasps. Not one wasp has been sighted here since. It also killed all the wallflowers and snapdragons. Many of the roses perished, and the furze died wholesale. It was a new light to us all that anything could kill gorse. The great bushes of it were withered to powder by the perpetual wind. That spring, we never had such swaling. The men burnt it all over the moor, hoping to save the roots for another year by getting rid of the dead boughs, which were killing the roots. Another curious danger was that we should have had next to no wool if the dead furze had been left. The prickles had been withered down to dry powder, and this filled the sheep's fleeces and one's dresses and everything that touched the bushes, and was absolutely impossible to remove from anything, even with a brush. So the men burnt and burnt and saved the wool and, we hope, the gorse too.

Another curious and aggravating feature of that winter was that we could dry no washing out of doors. In wet weather, we bear this with comparative composure, but in dry times with sun and wind it did seem maddening that you had not finished pegging out a line of washing before the first garment to be hung up was frozen stiff. I tried it till I was tired. The longer it was left out the harder it froze, and then when it was brought in at night it thawed, and was as wet as when it left the wash-tub.

One morning, Mrs. Bluejacket washed up the breakfast things, got a little water on her apron and went straight across the farm yard for the milk, returning at once. When she got in, she found that her apron had frozen stiff on her. I confess this depressed me. She had not been gone five minutes, and it seemed to be overdoing speed.

From that day I began to record temperatures. When I started, I disbelieved the thermometer, so got a second, but as they both said the same thing I was compelled to credit them with telling the truth.

I hung them in a north aspect, the bitterest I could find. The wind that winter was mostly north, with occasional spells of east. The thermometers hung in a northerly gale that stopped one's heart and made it jump like a dying fish when one first went out into the air, yet they never once got lower than twenty. This was three feet from the ground. At this time I also collected and measured icicles. By the stream here we had some, hanging to fronds of bracken, that were fifteen inches long and twenty inches in circumference. Some were evidently proud of a waist measure of twenty-six inches. Down along at the next farm, there was a wonderful sight; the sun one day melted a sprinkling of snow on the thatched roof and the frost caught the drippings as they fell. The whole length of that barn was decorated with a line of glittering pale gold icicles measuring three feet eleven inches. I never saw anything so utterly lovely. The farmer was obliged to get a long pole and knock the whole fringe to pieces lest the weight should damage the roof, and it was then he measured one. The Rainbow Maker stayed in bed for a few days, in and out, during the winter, as a formal protest against the weather clerk's behaviour, and one Sunday afternoon I held an ice exhibition in her room. I carried in a huge market basket of the most fantastic shapes I could find, and the ice was so hard and dry that it did not leak a drop. There were extraordinary fern effects of bracken fronds enclosed in crystal. The weirdest thing was a branch of wood almost too heavy to lift, and one wonderful ice helmet. The ice had settled round the top of a small boulder, making a perfect ice helmet with cockades at the side, rather the shape of a Wellington hat. It would have been the loveliest thing a fair woman ever put on her head, for the ice was as transparent as glass and all her hair would have shown through. But it was decidedly trickly about the edges, and was, moreover, a portentous weight.

Yet with all this, the thermometers never fell below twenty, even during the night. A portion of the winter, we had a very high barometer and flat calms, which meant phenomenal sun. I used to sit out for hours, grilling and revelling. The Rainbow Maker poisonously disapproves of this trick of mine. She never sits out and knows not how hot a winter sun can be. So in self-defence, one day, I took one of the thermometers to sit with me and put it on a twig in the hedge. I confess I was surprised at the result. It recorded one hundred, and many days ninety-eight. There was no snow and no refraction of heat from any surface. At the same hour, the porch thermometer in the wind registered twenty-two. I was so fired by these records that, incited by the kindness shown me when I wrote about an erring clock and watch, I sent a letter to the Meteorological office, saying I was aware that they had something better to do than to answer idle questions from irresponsible women on Dartmoor, but, if they had time, would they tell me whether this was a high sun record for England, and if it was usual to get such extremes of temperature in the same hour?

I received a polite reply from a Major of the R.E., who appeared to be in charge of the weather, and, to my great pride, he alluded to my record as a 'phenomenon' which, he said, was rare in England and was more like Davos, which made that climate such a despicable winter resort for invalids. I purred with joy at this official comparison of my beloved moor with Switzerland. It is curious why we get much higher sun temperatures proportionately in winter than in summer, but it is another proof of the divine beauty of our climate.

I have tried to get records from Torquay of this winter, but though I can find lowest shade temperature only four degrees ahead of us, I can find nothing about sun records. Until Torquay can produce authentic records of a higher sun temperature than one hundred – not in glass but in an open field – I shall continue to consider our climate a finer winter resort.

We do get such sun here in winter. My highest sun record in summer is one hundred and sixteen and sixty-five in the shade at the same hour. This is taken in a north wind when complete shelter from the wind was possible in a due south aspect: under the same conditions, therefore, as the winter records. But it illustrates what I say: that our winter sun is proportionately much hotter than our summer sun. Sixteen degrees between January and the dog-days is striking, and perhaps people will no longer wonder at the hours which I spend, grilling without a hat, in ice and snow.

✼

22
Rabbit Pie

The chance of the traditional goose for Christmas dinner was, for most on Dartmoor, an unlikely occurrence in times past. Neither was their holiday extended over a week or more as it is today. Even Boxing Day was a working day and Christmas day itself, for farmers, still meant cattle had to be fed, and cows had to be milked – as it does still. Tavistock Goose Fair, in October, was a major attraction but many a Dartmoor family relied upon rabbit – supposing winter had not decimated their population. A modern variation on this traditional meal comes from Jo Davies in Dartmoor – the Country Magazine.

DOUBLE CRUST RABBIT PIE

One Dartmoor tradition used to be the Boxing Day rabbit shoot, with pretty well all save the hunting fraternity participating. Again, rabbit farming – keeping rabbits in great warrens on the open moor – for both flesh and fur, used to play a major part in the local economy. Headland Warren (right in front of the Warren House Inn) is but one example. Young rabbits were roasted, older ones ended up in pies, stews or casseroles, cider frequently being added as a tenderising agent.

Ah, yes, cider... made in the off-moor lowlands and much traded for both grazing and labour, and proving all too addictive to some of 'they mortals'; to such an extent that, nectar of the gods of Dartmoor or not, the clergy are known to have prayed for the failure of the cider apple crop! Ingredients are as follows:

1 medium to large rabbit
6oz streaky bacon finely chopped
1 large onion finely chopped
1 average clove of garlic finely chopped
6oz mushrooms (sliced) OR 3oz dried mushrooms (rough-chopped)
quarter-pint cider
1oz butter
1oz flour
salt and pepper
half teaspoon mustard powder
1 level teaspoon grated nutmeg
2 bay leaves and a sprig or two of thyme
Threequarters of a pound flaky OR shortcrust pastry
1 beaten egg

Wash the rabbit, cut into seven or eight sensible pieces and leave immersed in salt water (1 level teaspoon salt) for two hours (this whitens the flesh), then drain and rinse well. Put the rabbit (including neck, heart, kidneys and liver, being careful to remove the bile sac in the case of this last item), all seasoning, nutmeg, bay and thyme in a pan, all but cover with water and simmer for 45 to 60 minutes. Leave to cool.

Carefully remove meat from bone and cut all the flesh (including the offal) into smallish pieces. Strain the stock, retaining half a pint and add this to the cider (to tenderise and enhance the flavour). Melt the butter in a frying-pan and add onion, garlic and bacon, cooking for a few minutes and stirring in the flour. Remove from heat and stir in stock a little at a time. Then return to heat and, still stirring (wooden spoon), bring to the boil and have the sauce thicken. Remove from heat, add rabbit and mushroom and check seasoning. Leave to cool.

Roll your pastry to about one-eighth inch thickness and line a pie dish. Damp the top edge all round, put in the filling and cover with a pastry lid which you seal, trim and flute. Use the trimmings for leaves and a rose (or whatever) for decoration, then brush with the beaten egg. Bake for 20 minutes at 425°F/220°C/Gas Mark 7 and then a further 20 minutes at 350°F/180°C/Gas Mark 4. Serve with creamed potatoes and seasonal vegetables.

✳

23
Winter warrener

William Crossing in his Dartmoor Worker *leaves a dramatic account of what was the final years of warrening on Dartmoor – essentially the harvesting of rabbits for food.*

It is a cheerless evening, and as you leave the warren house and feel the cold breath of air that sweeps down from the naked hills, you think what a pity it is they do not catch rabbits in the summer and during the daytime. But the warrener takes no notice of it. Carrying a huge bundle of nets he plods onward, followed by his assistant, who is laden in a similar manner. By-and-by you reach the beginning of a row of sticks, which have been stuck into the ground during the day, and the work of hanging up the nets commences. On one side of the row are some burrows, on the other are the rabbits. They have left their snug habitations to feed in quietness at night, and the warrener's first work is to take care that they shall not get back again.

The nets being hung the warrener returns to the house, which you do not feel particularly sorry for. When he calls you very early on the following morning you cannot help regretting that you have been so rash as to express a desire to go with him. But it is too late to retreat, and you rise and dress to the accompaniment of chattering teeth. Once more you make your way towards where the rabbits are feeding, and getting behind them drive them into the nets, being assisted in your work by spaniels. The warrener seizes the rabbits as they vainly endeavour to pass the nets, and kills them instantly by twisting their necks. When you look upon the heap of slain you are astonished.

The burrows, or burys, as the warrener calls them, are formed by first digging a narrow trench, with small ones branching from it on each side, but not opposite to each other. Large slabs of turf are then cut, and with these the little trenches are covered. Over this is heaped a mound of earth, and the burrow is finished. A few holes are made for the rabbits to enter, and they quickly take possession of their new abode.

During hard winters when food is scarce, the rabbits have to be fed, or they will leave the warren. This is a part of the warrener's work that has to be carefully attended to. Any neglect may result in considerable loss. The rabbits are usually fed on furze and hay.

The trapping season usually commences at the end of August or beginning of September, and lasts until the end of February or beginning of March. The warrens in the Plym valley find a market for their rabbits in Plymouth and Devonport, though from Ditsworthy many are sent to Birmingham. Birmingham and Sheffield are also markets for those caught in the warrens on the east side of the moor, the rabbits being dispatched from Moretonhampstead.

But the warrener's profits are declining. There are no such times now as those when the skin-packing at Ditsworthy was as important a matter as the wool-packing of an in-country farmer – when as much as £110 was received for skins in one year. Now that is over; the rabbits have to be sold in their skins, and much that once belonged to the warrener is lost to him. Prices are lower, too, than they were. Farmers take a great many rabbits to market now, and the warrener feels the competition. But what he has chiefly suffered from during late years is the scarcity of rabbits on the moor. In the great blizzard of 1891 thousands of rabbits died on Dartmoor, and the effect of the partial depopulation of the warrens in that year is still felt.

24
Riches in store

The Rev. Larkham was a Puritan minister in Tavistock following the Civil War and in his record of benefactions left by his parishioners reveals his less-than-simple tastes:

1653, Nov. 30th. The wife of Will Hodges brought me a fat goose. Lord, do them good! Edward Cole sent by his daughter a turkey; Lord, accept it! Dec. 2nd. Sara Trowt a dish of butter; accept, Lord! Dec. 6th. Margaret Sitwell would not be paid for 2lbs. of butter; is she not a daughter of Abraham? Father, be pleased to pay her. Walter Peek sent me, Dec. 14, a partridge, and W. Webb the same day pork and puddings; Lord, forget not! Mrs. Thomasin Doidge – Lord, look on her in much mercy – Dec. 19th gave me 5 shillings... Jan 25th. Mrs. Audry sent me a bushel of barley malt for housekeeping. Lord, smell a sweet savour! Patrick Harris sent me a shoulder of pork, – he is a poor ignorant man. Lord, pity him!

※

25
Providing for themselves

Poaching, among the nefarious trades, has an honourable tradition. But even at Christmas time poor folk stealing for the pot raises the eyebrow of Cecil Torr's grandfather writing in 1841.

On 13 December 1841 he writes: 'The poachers are catching the salmon – two have been taken in the meadow going to Lustleigh town, not large, about 10lbs. each. I hear many truff have been taken also. I believe they go further up, and are mostly taken by the Moreton men.' On 18 March 1844 he writes that Mr Wills of East Wrey is making a leet from the Wrey to irrigate his land. And on 9 April 1853 he writes: 'Mr Wills' man told me this week that they take up lots of fish on the grass at East Wrey that get out in irrigating the meadows, and that they took up one as big and long as his leg. I should say it was a salmon that went up at Candlemas: what they call Candlemas fish.'

And then on 8 April 1868 he writes 'No wonder the fish are scarce in our brook, for they have embankments for irrigation, which destroys such numbers of fish in spawning time that truff and white fish (bull-trout and salmon-trout) are rarely seen now. One of the old poachers tells me that he does not know of one being taken for three years past – except those that do succeed in going up are sure to be seen on the grass returning. Since my remembrance they had a free course up to Bughead in Moreton, and the Moreton fellows used to take them with their hands, and plenty left after. But all that is stopped: none to take.'

�֎

26
Pickled salmon

Salmon was once a common fish in Dartmoor's rivers and provided the poor with a nutritious supplement to their plain diet. The following recipe is a traditional one – presumably making a welcome change from poached fish!

Take salmon quite fresh, cut it in pieces but do not skin, boil it in water with a great deal of salt about a pint of vinegar to a salmon. When it is boiled leave it to drain till cold, season it very high with pepper, allspice, and pack it very close in with bay leaves among the layers, then have the top fastened down very close and put in tun-dish (a wooden cask). Fill the vessel with white wine and vinegar till the tun-dish is full, when you see any oil boil at top, skin it off clean and continue to do while it rises.

✖

27
Plum Pudding and Cider

Cecil Torr describes a Boxing Day feast. Plum puddings appear to figure large in the Christmas season diet.

There were immense plum puddings here at Christmas and also on all birthdays. My grandfather usually mentions them in his letters to my father. Thus, 26 December 1858, 'The men were here yesterday: goose and plum pudding as usual. Bob had the key of the cider cellar and was butler; so, depend on it, there was no lack of cider. However, they all left in good order.' Again, 4 January 1846, 'They were invited in yesterday on a famous piece of roasted pork and plum pudding, and drank the little creature's good health. I believe they would be glad if Baby's birthday came every month.' And again, 3 January 1869, 'Plum puddings have followed pretty quick of late, but there will be a cessation till April, if my life is spared till that time: if not, of course, no pudding.'

⁂

28
Plum Cake

One suspects that our proprietory Christmas puddings are but a pale shadow of the kind of fare served up by our predecessors. Just look at the ingredients in this Victorian recipe for Plum Cake.

Mix thoroughly a quarter of a peck of fine flour well dried, with a pound of dry and sifted loaf sugar, three pounds of currants washed, and very dry, half a pound of raisins stoned and chopped, a quarter of an ounce of mace and cloves, twenty Jamaica peppers, a grated nutmeg, the peel of a lemon cut as fine as possible, and half a pound of almonds blanched and beaten with orange flower water. Melt two pounds of butter in a pint and a quarter of cream, but not hot, put to it a pint of sweet wine, a glass of brandy, the whites and yolks of twelve eggs beaten apart, and half a pint of good yeast. Strain this liquid by degrees into the dry ingredients, beating them together a full hour, then butter the hoop or pan, and bake it. As you put the batter into the hoop, or pan, throw in plenty of citron, lemon and orange candy.

If you ice the cake, take half a pound of double-refined sugar sifted, and put a little with the white of an egg, beat it well, and by degree pour in the remainder. It must be whisked near an hour, with the addition of a little orange-flower water, but mind not to put much. When the cake is done, pour the icing over and return it to the oven for fifteen minutes; but if the oven be warm, keep it near the mouth, and the door open, lest the colour be spoiled.

❋

29
No pudding

Again Cecil Torr:

My grandfather writes to my father, 18 March 1844, 'I remember going to see old — of Crediton about some business, and was sitting down by the fire talking with him, when a great coarse country maid came in and disturbed us. The old man was quite in a rage to see the maid tumbling everything over, and asked what she wanted. She said, 'Why, us have lost the pudding-cloth six weeks, and as the gentleman is going to dine here, I suppose us shall have a pudding now.' Turning round to me, the old man said corn was so dear, he could not afford to have puddings. He was a rich old man, grandfather of — and —. I once asked him What news (as he was reading a paper) and he replied, 'Oh, I don't know: my paper is a fortnight old: I get it for a ha'penny then'.

30
Pursuing the inedible

Hunting was a Yuletide custom for all. Boxing Day meets were tremen-
dously popular in past times, and even today they are attended by
hundreds of spectators, supporters – and protestors. In The Hound and
the Horn, *W. F. Collier describes the life of his friend, the huntsman*
Harry Terrell (1807–1871).

There was an old fox-hunter, a great authority with the Dartmoor,
and had been a good man in his day, who was always engaged in a
wordy war with Terrell about sporting and everything else, carried
on with very good temper, more, perhaps, for the fun of Terrell's talk
than for anything else.

When this old gentleman laid down the law, which he was apt to
do, Terrell would tell him he was 'past', and could not see a hound
either in covert or in chase, which was true enough. We were drawing a young plantation on the borders of the moor, with under-
growth of furze as thick as a mat.

Terrell said, 'Give 'em time, 'tis very thick.'

The old gentleman as usual contradicted him, and said, 'Not a bit
of it. Do you call that thick?'

Terrell said, 'I'll bet ee ten shillings you wan't get through un in
twenty minutes.'

The covert was not more than two or three acres.

'Done,' said the old gentleman.

I held the stakes, and the old gentleman got off his horse, which
Terrell held, and proceeded in breeches and boots to struggle
through the covert, and I held my watch to note the time.

It was so thick the old gentleman could scarcely get through, but
he had plenty of pluck, and by working very hard, he appeared at
the opposite side in nineteen minutes. I thought at his age he never
would have got out of that gorse at all.

The rest of the field had gone on, and I remained with Terrell,
watch and stakes in hand. When I handed over the money, the old
gentleman said, 'Stop, I can't get on my horse yet.'

Terrell's laugh was worth hearing. It was blowing a cold cutting

Huntsmen on the Green at Manaton c.1900.

wind from the east on an exposed bit of moor, and the old gentle-man had to completely strip his lower limbs and bare them to the blast to pick out the prickles from his breeches, whilst Terrell held his horse, congratulating him on his having won his bet, and saying he would not go through it, himself, for ten shillings on any account.

He seemed to think the ten shillings well laid out.

It was at least ten minutes before the old gentleman could mount his horse, and he was in misery the rest of the day, not relieved by Terrell's ridicule.

3
BIRDS AND BEASTS

31
The Robin

Inextricably linked with Christmas, the unmistakable robin is common on the borders of the moor. This poem, by Woodhouse Lane, first appeared in Dartmoor in Devon and Other Poems *in 1918.*

WELCOME! cheery little friend,
Bright and bold and merry,
What a pretty breast you have,
As red as any berry.

You are a trusting little bird
Few other birds are able
To brave the terrors of a room,
And hop upon our table.

From dawn to dusk you sing your song
In the bleakest weather,
And only stop to feed or fight,
Or preen a ruffled feather.

You seem to love the winter well,
The hoar-frost and the snow,
The shelter of the holly-tree,
The bunch of mistletoe.

You are the sprite of Christmas
A kind of fairy Puck,
Who never lets a mortal pass
Without his share of luck.

So, here's a toast, my merry friend
'May you win a sprightly wife,
And own six baby robins,
And live a jolly life.'

32
Unwelcome winter visitor

For those living on Dartmoor a sudden appearance of mice in the autumn is nothing unusual, particularly in homes with thatched roofs. The occasional scrabbling in the attic can be kept at bay with traps but these winter invasions are usually harmless. On the other hand, as Cecil Torr points out, a rat is less welcome.

One winter afternoon I went up to my bedroom and found a rat there, sitting on the rug before the fire. It did not move when I came in, but looked at me appealingly. I understood, and it saw I understood; and we had as clear a conversation as if we had expressed ourselves in words. The rat said, ' I must apologize for this unwarranted intrusion; but I am suffering from some distressing malady, and entertain a hope that it may be within your power to alleviate my sufferings.' I said, 'I regret exceedingly that this should be entirely beyond my powers. I know too little of human maladies, and even less of the maladies of rodents; and were I to adopt the treatment usually prescribed for them, I fear your sufferings might be aggravated.' And the rat said, ' You disappoint me grievously. But at least, I trust, you will not abuse the confidence I have reposed in you?' I said, 'Nothing could be further from my thoughts,' and held the door politely open. The rat walked slowly out, stopped at the top of the stairs, and looked back at me with much more confidence, 'But really isn't there anything at all that you can do for me?' I said, 'I'm awfully sorry, but I'm afraid there isn't.' And the rat went slowly downstairs, out of doors, and away along the Pixey Garden.

33
A Farmer's Lot

Winter demands great fortitude from the moorland farmer. The sudden changes of weather on Dartmoor can catch out even the most wary. The care of stock is paramount when the weather takes a sudden turn for the worse. Susan Haughton, whose family farmed at Wingstone, records in The Book of Manaton *the Big Freeze of 1962.*

The snow started 28 December 1962 with a terrific blizzard that filled the drive with snow, it snowed the next day with bitter winds and freezing conditions and again on 3 January. The snow came halfway up the french windows on the verandah. There was no water, and we got it from the stream and the well, drinking water came in a churn from the Kestor Inn. Water came back mid January. We had 180 sheep in the yard; a narrow path was cleared down to the Mill and up the road to the Green and down the drive. The sheep were walked along this to give them exercise as they were in lamb. More heavy blizzards came on 2, 4, 5 February, and the road to Bovey was cut off. There was still snow hanging about in the second week in March.

Most people needed cattle and sheep fodder, but the blizzards meant that helicopters could not be used. A huge 4 wheel-drive army lorry came to us and it got stuck in the yard, and was winched up the drive on the beech trees, one tree at a time.

The sheep in the yard used to be against the door, and they fell in when you tried to open it. More than once my father, who was a slight man, was carried along on the backs of the sheep, with buckets flying everywhere at feeding time.

When it finally thawed, a local farmer and his son took the muck out of the yard and it was two feet thick.

At the worst of the freeze, I found a cow, not ours, on the road absolutely frozen stiff, it was still breathing and couldn't move, even though it was standing up. The owner came with bales of straw, and rubbed her all over until he could move her.

It was actually a very beautiful time, and once the blizzards stopped the sun came out. Until the roads were cleared, anyone

Delivering milk by sledge in Manaton during the winter of 1945.

who had a Land Rover would shop for everyone else. People who didn't normally go to the pub, all walked there, and it brought the village together.

People who lived up at the Laneside and Southcott area, would walk to the village on top of the hedges.

We milked 18 Jerseys, and kept big flat pans of milk in the larder and skimmed the lovely yellow cream off, and sometimes had it on our cornflakes. The milk was taken up to the top of the drive in churns. We had to sell the dairy cows when we had more beef cattle, as we were not allowed the beef subsidy if we were milking.

The cattle were mainly Galloways with an Angus bull, but sometimes we hired a Hereford bull from the Shilstons at Torhill farm. We had Scotch Blackface sheep when we started, but spent all our time looking for them, so then we went to Devon Closewool, and a few Dorset Horns.

※

34
Late swallows

Though we imagine winters past were more severe, the truth is they had
mild seasons too. Even so, Eliza Bray's reports of house martins staying
on until Christmas in Devon seem extraordinary:

I here also may add (as another proof of the mildness of our air) the
following particulars, which I have seen stated in Dr. Moore's cata-
logue, lately published, of the birds of Devon. The Doctor says, 'Of
the house swallow, or martin, I have seen the old birds feeding their
young on the 20th of September, 1828, at Warleigh; and have been
assured, by a good observer, that martins have frequently been seen
flying during mild weather even in the *Christmas week*, at
Plympton.'

Our winters are seldom severe; and when we have snow it does
not lie long upon the ground. But Dartmoor, from its great eleva-
tion, is far more liable to snow-storms and hard weather than we are,
who live in a less elevated country. Mr. Bray recollects that, when
he was a boy, returning from school at Christmas, three men with
shovels went before the carriage as it crossed the Moor, in order to
remove the snow-heaps which, in particular places, would otherwise
have rendered it impassable.

✱

35
The Dartmoor Pony

In recent times it has been suggested that, through want of any
commercial value, ponies may disappear altogether from the moor.
William Crossing in One Hundred Years on Dartmoor *records that*
threats to the existence of these animals are not new.

In the early part of 1880, and again in 1881, there were very heavy
falls of snow on Dartmoor, and access to many of the farms was
rendered impossible for days together. The winter of 1885–6 was

Dartmoor ponies are expert at foraging – eating almost anything that grows on the moor, including the spiky tips of gorse bushes.

also a very hard one, and the ponies suffered terribly. During the spring of 1886 we saw a number of carcasses of these animals on the Moor; there have been few years in which the severity of the weather has occasioned so great a loss. Unfortunately many of these animals are kept by persons who have no land in the 'in-country,' and thus being unable to drive them to a place of shelter, it not infrequently happens that they are left to suffer from the fury of the storm, and when the herbage is covered with snow for any length of time, to starve.

Hardy though the Dartmoor pony may be, there are certain times in the depth of winter when it would be but humane for the owners to gather them in, for when the storm does not give sufficient warning to enable this to be done, it could generally be accomplished when the snow is down. From the point of view of self-interest this would be wise, but the higher motive should never be wanting.

✳

36
Pony express

Reg Bellamy, author of the book Postbridge - The Heart of Dartmoor, *describes some of the difficulties that heavy snowfalls caused in delivering the mail. His father, Jack, became known as 'the Postman on a pony'.*

That year there were heavy snow storms and it was suggested that gratuities be paid to sub-postmasters, postmen and contractors, on a sliding scale of ten shillings downwards, for getting the mail through from Yelverton and Princetown. An allowance for a shelter for a postman at Postbridge was refused in 1899.

Jack Bellamy delivering the mail.

The Warren Inn delivery was increased in frequency in 1903, and in 1905 it was extended to Golden Dagger Mine. Deliveries to Bellever were increased to 3 days a week in 1907.

In 1909 the Yelverton–Princetown mail cart service was extended to Postbridge and I think it must have been about this time that mail was sorted at Postbridge, with two Auxiliary postmen employed on deliveries, for in 1911 arrangements were made for deliveries to Laughter Farm and House. They were: April–October daily delivery; November March 3-days a week, on Mondays, Wednesdays and Fridays. In 1917 the Yelverton–Postbridge cart service was discontinued and the mail transferred by rail to Princetown.

✖

37
The Dartmoor greyhound

That there might be distinct types of fox may seem strange to those who think of Reynard as being a singular animal, instantly recognisable even when glimpsed only for a second or two. To William Crossing and his forebears, however, foxes had differing regional identities, even within the borders of the moor.

This district was also the scene of the operations of Tom French, of Widecombe, who early in the 19th century waged war against the foxes in the neighbourhood of his home. According to the Rev. E. W. L. Davies, the author of *Dartmoor Days*, Mr. John Bulteel is said to have turned loose a number of French and English foxes on Dartmoor. The farmers around Widecombe suffering considerably from their depredations, it was decided that endeavours should be made to exterminate them, and to Tom French was the task entrusted. To this he applied himself diligently, hunting the 'varmints' with a few hounds and terriers, and when, after a long time, he found that he had gained the end in view, he also discovered that he had acquired a great liking for the chase. There being now no further support from the farmers, Tom's occupation was gone, but he was still determined upon the gratification of his new taste. He soon became an ardent follower of hounds, and was always a great favourite with the gentlemen of the hunt.

Possibly the descendants of some of the animals which Tom French at first so ruthlessly pursued are still found on the Moor. At all events, the fox in the southern portion of Dartmoor is said to be of Continental extraction, and is often spoken of as a French fox. He is different in appearance from the fox of northern Dartmoor, being smaller and of a redder colour. Mr. C. A. Harris describes the Moor fox of the latter district as high on leg, wiry, and powerful; a most redoubtable customer to meet at any time, and an animal unknown to the eastward. 'He is not to be handled after a thirty minutes' burst, but requires a long, stern chase at very great speed.'

As pointed out in the chapter on wild quadrupeds in Rowe's *Perambulation*, 'the necessity for travelling long distances and the rough climate has led, by the survival of the fittest, in the matter of foxes, to the formation of almost a special breed in the Dartmoor highlands, having distinct peculiarities.' Among hunting men this fox is known as the Dartmoor greyhound.

38
A harmless life

The Rev. Baring-Gould (1834-1924) was a prolific author and avid collector of folk songs. He travelled the Westcountry listening to local people singing, writing down the words and music he heard, which now comprise a valued and unique collection. He was not above changing words or music, however, where he thought fit. In the following song – collected from a man named Cole who worked in the quarries at Merrivale – the tale is told of a deer that escaped from Elford Park, Yelverton.

THE SILLY DOE

Give ear unto my mournful song
Gay huntsmen every one,
And unto you I will relate

My sad and doleful moan.
O here I be a silly Doe,
From Elford Park I strayed,
In leaving of my company
Myself to death betrayed.
The master said I must be slain
For 'scaping from his bounds:
'O keeper, wind the hunting horn,
And chase him with your hounds.'
A Duke of royal blood was there,
And hounds of noble race;
They gathered in a rout next day,
And after me gave chase.
They roused me up one winter morn,
The frost it cut my feet,
My red, red blood came trickling down,
And made the scent lie sweet.
For many a mile they did me run,
Before the sun went down,
Then I was brought to give a teen,
And fall upon the groun'.
The first rode up, it was the Duke:
Said he, 'I'll have my will!'
A blade from out his belt he drew
My sweet red blood to spill.
So with good cheer they murdered me,
As I lay on the ground;
My harmless life it bled away,
Brave huntsmen cheering round.

39
Hawthorn and Holly

Cecil Torr upon the decline in country lore:

Mild winters often end with falls of snow in March or April – at any rate, it is so here – and this must be the basis of the saw, 'A green Christmas, a white Easter.' My Grandfather quotes it on 28 December 1857 as 'an old adage – I fear it may be too true.' On 12 January 1862 he writes, 'How mild it is. Well, this verifies the saying of old that if the hawthorn and holly berries are plenty, be sure of a hard winter, but if none, a mild one; and there is scarcely a berry to be seen, even on our hollies which are generally so thick. When I was young these sayings were more general than now; and it is considered that the alwise Providence is mindful of the birds as well as man.'

※

40
Bad luck

Robert Herrick in Hesperides *(1848) warns of the dangers in leaving Christmas decorations up in the house:*

> *Down with the rosemary, and so,*
> *Down with the baies and misletoe;*
> *Down with the holly, ivie, all,*
> *Wherewith you drest the Christmas hall:*
> *That so the superstitious find*
> *No one least branch there left behind.*
> *For look how many leaves there be*
> *Neglected there (maids, trust to me),*
> *So many goblins you shall see.*

※

41
Mild winters...

Cecil Torr:

The birds come down here from the bleaker country round the moor as soon as wintry weather sets in, and the ground below the hollies is red with berries that the birds have dropped. But this last winter was so mild that no birds came, though berries were more abundant than ever was known before. In another such winter my grandfather writes, 25 January 1846, 'I cannot find any of the old men I meet can ever recollect such a mild winter, so far. I have not yet seen a winter's bird, not a fieldfare or starling or even a whindle [redwing] nor a covey of birds of any description: neither the linnet nor finch nor yellowhammer have congregated together as heretofore: they are all about singly as in summer. They do not appear to want the food of the barn's door, the cornricks, or stable court, so far. Hope it is all for a wise purpose.'

✳

42
...and hard winters

Of course, there sometimes are hard winters here, as in 1907, when almost all the birds were killed; and he writes, 14 May 1855, 'Birds of all sorts are very scarce, the winter made great havoc of them: not a thrush to be heard nor a blackbird to be seen. I have not a robin in the garden.' But winters of that kind are rare.

4
STORM AND FLOOD

43
The rain it raineth

Of course it is the rainfall that sets Dartmoor apart from the rest of the county, its average of around 60 inches per annum being almost twice that of Torquay, and with Princetown averaging a coat-soaking 85 inches. Mrs Bray's view is not an understatement:

The atmosphere of Dartmoor deserves particular notice; it is nearly always humid. The rain, which frequently falls almost without intermission for many weeks together, is generally small; and resembles more a Scotch mist than a shower. Sometimes, however, it will pour down in torrents; but storms attended with thunder and lightning are not very common: and whenever they do occur, one would think that the peasantry still retained the superstitious awe of the aboriginal inhabitants of the Moor, who worshipped thunder as a god under the name of Tiranis.

�֎

44
Tiranis Rex

Mrs Bray is right too about thunder. According to Dartmoor: A New Study *there are on average 7.3 days per annum when thunder occurs – but when lightning strikes (see entry 8) it often has disastrous results. A report in the* Western Morning News *of 15 August 1933 is typical:*

Rock House, Morwell Down (Tavistock), the residence of Mr Taylor, was struck by lightning on Sunday night. It was about 10pm when Mr and Mrs Taylor were downstairs that a terrible thud was heard,

Eight bullocks killed by lightning at Princetown, 4 September 1913.

and Mr Taylor, on running upstairs, found plastering and pieces of wood littering the landing on the top storey, while a wardrobe on the same landing was alight and there was also a small fire in the attic adjoining.

When the police went to use the fire alarm they found the wires had been fused and so personal calls had to be made to the firemen.

Meanwhile Constables Bateford, Marshall and Parnell went with the Tavistock ambulance men to the scene, but on arrival found that the fire had been got under control.

During the storm on Sunday night a cow was killed by lightning on a farm about five miles from Bradninch.

✳

44
Lost bridges

Thunderstorms are more commonly associated with July and August and the great flood of July 1890 in the Tavy, Walkham and Cowsic valleys swept away a number of bridges, including the ancient clapper over the Cowsic. However, many destructive winter storms are also on record, as William Crossing relates:

Considerable destruction has at times been wrought by storms and floods on the moor, and of these the 19th century has witnessed many. On the 27th January, 1823, the Plym and the Mew, or Meavy River, rose at night to an immense height, the combined torrents reaching to the keystone of Shaugh Bridge – not the present structure, but an older one which it has replaced. It is said, but this is probably an exaggeration, that so great was the volume of water in the Plym that the spray was flung over the Dewerstone, which rises to no inconsiderable height above the river.

In November, 1824, a terrific storm was experienced, when so great was the force of the wind that some large stones on the summit of Brent Hill were carried to a considerable distance. On the 13th of May, 1839, and two following days, there was a sharp frost and heavy falls of snow on and around the moor, the ground in many places being covered to a great depth.

During the Christmas season of 1841 a tempest arose, the ravages of which on the western side of the moor were said to be quite fearful. The little river Burn, which rises near where Lydford Station now is, and flows between Black Down and the Heathfield, so rapidly overflowed its banks that in half an hour the valley near the farm of Wringworthy presented all the appearance of a lake. The house was inundated, and the cattle were only saved by the prompt exertions of the inhabitants.

In 1873 a flood unfortunately swept away a clapper bridge that spanned the Blackabrook, a tributary of the West Dart. This bridge was near Fice's Well, a little edifice of 16th century erection, and which is situated in the tract of ground now belonging to the Prison, and lying north of the road between Rundle Stone Corner and Two Bridges. The bridge possessed a more than ordinary interest, inasmuch as it indicated the direction of an old track across this part of the Forest.

※

45
Lydford bridge

So common are tales of lost bridges on the moor that they would make a book in themselves. Perhaps the best-known of all such tales is the story of the fallen bridge at Lydford:

There are few scenes in Devonshire so remarkable as this. One comes along an ordinary country lane, for here the soil is not waste, but cultivated, and dropping down a little hill the bridge lies straight in front, looking in no wise different from any ordinary piece of stonework that carries a country road across a rustic brook, until one stands upon it. Then it is seen that the valley below is not only exceptionally deep, but that in the bottom of its richly wooded slope the stream has cut down straight and sheer a deep black gorge through the solid rocks, where it thunders on in shadow, far beyond the reach of sunlight, a gloomy torrent in whose sound the steady singing of the moorland streams is deepened into a harsh threatening roar. When rain has sent the water boiling furiously down this gorge, there is a distinct note of terror in the sound; and even when the water is low, it runs along with none of that soft splashing which tempts one to linger on the bridge at Tavistock, but has a sulky murmur mingled with an occasional deep sucking noise as if the water had swirled into some deep hole and torn itself out again by sheer impetuosity and force. The gorge is deep enough to be majestic. Here and there a tree lies prostrate over it.

Once long ago a traveller was riding by night from Tavistock to Lydford. There was a wild storm; the floods were out in the valleys; the wind blew as it seldom does except on Dartmoor; and the traveller kept his horse at a steady gallop, as far as the roughness of the roads permitted, being anxious at finding himself overtaken by darkness in a country with which he was unacquainted. Those who know the ground will understand that he must have been a bold rider to go at any but handpace in so violent a storm, but he persevered, and at length his horse gave a tremendous spring which made him think he must have leapt a hedge, and darted panting up towards the lights of Lydford, which at that moment came in sight

The bridge at Lydford showing the precipitous drop into the gorge below.

upon the hill. In five minutes more the tired traveller was dismounting, and answering as patiently as possible the ordinary questions as to where he had come from. 'From Tavistock,' he said. 'But the bridge is down!' they replied incredulously; and when morning came they led him back and showed him a broken arch spanning half way across the awful chasm, and the swollen torrent roaring far below among the mass of broken stonework, on which both he and his horse would have been dashed to pieces had they failed in a leap which no man would have dared to attempt in daylight.

✳

46
Local rivalry

Perhaps it was after the storm witnessed by Crossing that the following event, described by Rev. Baring-Gould, occurred:

One day after a storm of rain the River Tavy rolled down volumes of water, and a poor wretch was caught by the flood on a rock in midstream; he was unable to reach the bank. He screamed for assistance. Presently a man came along the other side and halted, and called to the fellow in danger, 'I say, be you a Peter Tavy or a Mary Tavy man?' 'Peter Tavy', answered the wretch in danger. 'Throw me a rope, or I shall be drowned.' 'No, no', answered he on the land, 'I be a Mary Tavy man; so go on hollering till a Peter Tavy chap comes by'; and he left the fellow in distress to his fate.

✳

47
The spectral lovers

Of the many ghost stories associated with the moor, this tale of two lovers forever separated by the waters of a cascading stream is perhaps the most poignant. Recounted by William Crossing in Gems in a Granite Setting *it is a folktale that has resonances in many other parts of the country.*

Beardown clapper bridge - swept away in the great flood of 1890.

About half a mile down the Lich Path crosses the river at Willsworthy Ford and here, according to a story, a spectre horseman may be seen whenever the moon lights up a stormy sky, and the usually bright stream comes down from the hills a raging torrent. It is said that long ago a lady was wont to come to meet her lover secretly at the ford. Who she was is not recorded: we only know that she was young and beautiful, wore rich apparel, rode a splendid white horse, and dwelt in the neighbourhood of Lydford. We also know little about the lover, further than that he, too, was young, and also very handsome, dressed in a fashionable style, rode a magnificent black steed, and made his home in the Forest of Dartmoor. The story intimates that they met clandestinely because of the lady's father, who was so unreasonable as to wish to choose a husband for his daughter, instead of allowing her to do so herself. This is rather puzzling, because in such cases we almost invariably find that the suitor to whom the lady has given her heart is poor, whereas in the present instance the presumption is that he was wealthy. Had it been otherwise he could hardly have possessed a valuable steed, or have been able to dress in the most fashionable style, as the story says he did. How he contrived to learn the latest mode in the Forest of Dartmoor it is difficult to understand, but, as a native of the Moor once said to me, 'there's no knawin' what vokes doo'd yeers agone,' and so we will content ourselves with what the story relates concerning him.

The youthful lover was always the first to arrive at the ford, and there he would await the coming of the beautiful girl who had ensnared his heart, never crossing the stream until he saw her descending the rugged path that led to the bank. It was agreed that their meetings should take place towards the close of the day, and never did the lady fail to appear before the western hills hid the sun. But one evening her lover saw the rosy luminary go down behind a great bank of storm clouds, tinging the edges of the inky masses with a fierce red, and still she came not. An hour passed by, and darkness began to usher in the night, but yet the youth lingered by the stream. Suddenly the moaning of the wind ceased, and the signs that had portended the coming tempest were verified. Then out of the silence, broken only by the sighs of the river that rose from the rocky cleave up the valley, came the loud crash of thunder, and presently the laden clouds poured their watery burden upon the darkened earth. Awhile the storm lasted, and then a calm fell upon all around, and a deep hush again rested over the moor upon which the moon looked down through the swiftly fleeting vapours that partially veiled her. Soon another sound struck upon the ear of the youth who, no shelter being near, had been constrained to brave the fury of the elements. It grew louder, and by-and-bye the stream at his feet became agitated, and rose so rapidly that it speedily covered the stepping-stones near the ford. Then with a mighty rush a wall of water appeared, and in a few moments the Tavy's banks were swept by an angry flood.

The young lover succeeded in reaching a place of safety, but he had hardly done so when the dim light of the moon showed him the form of her he had come to meet. She was galloping down the old Lich Path towards the ford, but reined in her horse as she neared the bank and saw the swollen river before her. On its verge she stopped, and looked about as though to find a place where she might cross. Her lover tried to warn her of her danger, but his voice was drowned in the roar of the stream. Then two horsemen appeared, furiously riding down the ancient way by which she had come. No sooner did she perceive them than she urged her steed forward, and the white horse plunged fearlessly into the turbulent waters. But he was powerless against their mad onrush, and was rapidly carried away by the current, while his fair rider was swept from the saddle. For an instant her lover saw her pale face and one uplifted arm, and their eyes met. Then she went down beneath the surging flood, and the father who would have forced her to wed with one she could not love, and the man who would have taken her while aware that her heart was another's, knew that they had driven her to her death.

The white horse gained the bank at a point lower down the stream, and on that side of it which his mistress had hoped to reach. While yet the misty moon shed a dim light upon the moor, a rider passed over the Lich Path, his face set towards the Forest. The steed he rode moved across the heath like a dark shadow; one which he led resembled, in that faint light, a pale ghost.

Years passed by, when one night a traveller reaching Willsworthy Ford, saw by the light of the moon that the Tavy was in flood, and not to be crossed. As he was turning away towards the bridge down the stream, he was terror stricken at seeing the shadowy figure of a young man mounted on a black horse and leading a white one, suddenly appear on the bank. The steeds moved silently along the margin of the flood, the man, who wore a richly laced coat beneath a heavy riding cloak, seeming to peer into it as though in search of something. When the traveller related his story he was not believed, but by-and-bye the spectre horseman was again seen, and more than once, but only when the moon looked down upon the Tavy and saw an angry river. Then those in the neighbourhood knew that the spirit of the youthful lover haunted the spot where the beautiful girl whose heart he had won had perished.

5
A CHRISTMAS TALE

I remember looking out on a cold Christmas eve. The sky was black beyond the lights of the village. Stars appeared behind the gathering clouds and one, brighter than the rest, twinkled in the bare branches of the swaying ash trees. It was cold.

My wife, nine months and a couple of days pregnant, sat before the dying fire, a book resting on the bulge she'd carried around since summer. She caught the anxious look I gave her as I drew the curtains. She smiled.

'Perhaps I'd better phone.'

'Is it snowing?' she asked.

'No, but I think it might. Better to be safe... .'

'Than sorry?'

We both smiled.

'I'm sure nothing will happen tonight.' She gave her stomach a reassuring pat. 'Anyway, unless it snows really hard, we'll still get the car through.'

'Famous last words.' I grimaced and stirred a log into life on the fire. 'Are you sure?'

'Certain.'

We should have known. Where having a baby is concerned few things are certain. That night the wind piled cloud pillows over the sleeping village and while we slept snowflakes crept stealthily out of the sky.

'Are you awake?'

I woke with a start. 'Almost.'

'I think it's started,' Mary whispered, sounding frightened in the dark. I turned on the light and she was half-sitting up in the bed, pale faced.

'I'll phone.' I pushed the covers aside and swung my feet on to the chilly floor.

'Yes.'

It was almost three. Snow lay deep and was still falling. Flakes whirled out of the night and crashed silently against the window. I heard Mary moving upstairs.

'It's snowing,' I called. Then softly so she wouldn't hear. 'Hard.'

Even with an inch or two of snow the road up to the village was almost impassable. At night, and in a blizzard, there was little hope of our car managing the trip – less chance of an ambulance getting through. Even before I lifted the phone I had bargained for that eventuality, but what I did not expect was that the phone would not be working at all. I stared at it in disbelief. And Mary at the foot of the stairs stared at me.

Mary sank into the chair before the dying fire.

'Do you think...?'

'I'm sure,' she nodded. Her face white and anxious.

'I'll go to the village. Use the kiosk.' I said, as brightly as possible.

Of course that phone line was down too. Nor would a mobile work in the folds of the valley where the village, white and silent, lay in darkness beneath the falling snow. I stood for a minute bathed in a pool of yellow light from the phone box, blew on my fingers and stamped my freezing feet. The only other light visible came from our cottage. I thought of Mary alone and afraid.

In nearby houses, eaves already piled with snow, parents had long ago completed their Christmas vigil, creeping into bedrooms and placing laden stockings gently at the foot of sleeping beds.

Strangers are not easily accepted in rural communities, even today, and a black doctor is treated with more suspicion than most. Newly arrived in our village he had yet to earn the friendly trust that we had come to take for granted.

It was hard-going through the narrow lanes, icy wind stinging my face, snow flakes battering my eyes. Hesitating, I knocked on the doctor's door, too quietly at first, then urgently as I thought again of Mary at home and alone.

A light came on, door bolts rattled and a black face appeared around the door's edge.

'My wife,' I pointed aimlessly into the darkness behind me. 'She's having a baby.'

The doctor nodded and undid the heavy chain securing the door. He too was suspicious of the natives.

'Come in. I'll get some things I need.'

The doctor and I struggled up the hill together back into the village. Mary lay on the bed, fear in her eyes and perspiration on her forehead. She smiled at the doctor who took her hand gently in his. He then looked at me.

'You better make yourself a cup of tea,' he said. 'You look dreadful.'

It was six-thirty when the baby arrived. Outside the snow continued to fall. Inside a row of cats and a dog watched as the doctor and I drank tea at the kitchen table. Mary slept and our new son slept too. The doctor and I talked until dawn and he left waving a bottle of scotch I had pressed upon him. I watched as he inched his way carefully down the path – a black man in a world of white.

Mary slept until ten. By then the snow had stopped and the smoke from village chimneys rose in thin columns above the rooftops.

'He doesn't look like you.' Mary said, holding up the baby for me to see. A little face peered from the folds of a blanket, tiny fingers clutching mine.

I was feeding the cats when the first of our visitors arrived. The Professor called 'hello' from the hall and stamped his feet to rid his boots of snow.

'I hear glad tidings,' he laughed. 'I hope all's well.' I shook his hand and he patted my shoulder. We had known the Professor for a long time. For all his seventy years and forgetful habits he was a youthful man, and kind too.

'A present for you.' He handed me a badly wrapped box of cigars.

'Thanks.'

'Actually I'd sort of forgotten about you. Is Mary awake?'

I watched the old man as Mary handed him our child and he took him gently in his arms. He smiled, but could not hide a sadness in his eyes, and joy too. Tears stained his face. In that moment none of us could speak.

The Professor handed Mary a present. A small earthenware pot which she held up for me to see. 'What is it?' she asked him.

'Perfume. Got it in Egypt. Had it for years. Actually its frankincense.'

We forgot Christmas lunch. The turkey stayed in the fridge. Outside it began to snow again and there was no sign of a thaw. I made up the fire while Mary dozed upstairs and was settling down with a book when our second visitor arrived. It was the doctor.

He looked over Mary and the baby, appearing downstairs a few minutes later, nodding his approval.

'Both fine,' he smiled. He declined a drink and took the snowy path homewards.

Mary was sitting up in bed. Our son asleep beside her.

'Look.' She held up a small green bottle. 'The doctor gave it to me. It comes from Africa.'

Mary caught the look of confusion on my face.

'It's not medicine, silly. It's a present.'

I took the emerald green bottle and removed the glass stopper. A musty and mysterious fragrance greeted my nostrils.

'Blimey, what's that?'

'You're not going to believe this.'

'What?'

'It's myrrh.'

Much later, from a window, I watched solitary snowflakes falling idly from the evening sky. Lights shone from houses in the village, and children's shouts drifted in the cold still air. I watched as our third visitor struggled slowly up the hill, picking his way on spindly legs between the deeper drifts. Old Tom lived alone in a caravan at the edge of the village; had done for years. His grubbiness thinly disguised a heart of gold.

I opened the door to him as he reached the step and he looked up at me, head on one side.

'Cain't stop,' he coughed and thumped his chest.

'Just for minute, Tom. Come in.'

He peered through the doorway and sniffed.

'Naw. Cain't stop,' he repeated, glancing over his shoulder. 'Them blighters is throwin' snowballs.' He jabbed a dirty thumb in the direction of the village square.

'Stop for a minute. Have a drink.'

'Naw,' said Tom, who *was* a drinking man. 'Your missus. She 'ad a baby?'

'Yes, come inside.' I was beginning to get cold.

'Cain't stop. Brought this for the little un.' And from his pocket he drew a crumpled slip of paper, and thrust it towards me, before turning on his heels.

'Thanks Tom.' I called after him. 'I'll give your present to Mary.'

He turned for a second, hopping on one leg in the snow like a tattered crow. 'It's for the baby.'

'Who was that?' Mary asked sleepily.

'Old Tom. He brought a present for the baby.' I handed her the paper.

Mary looked at the package and unwrapped it.

'There,' she said, holding out her palm towards me, 'it's a pound coin.' She leaned over to show it to the sleeping baby.

I sat on the bed and kissed Mary on her forehead.

'I know what you're thinking,' I said.

'Silly, isn't it,' she gently replied.

Next day the phone lines were repaired and by late morning snow-ploughs had reached the village reconnecting us with the world outside. But our lives were never to be quite the same again.